CHANGE

Hellmut Wilhelm

CHANGE

Eight Lectures on the *I Ching*

Translated from the German
by Cary F. Baynes

Routledge & Kegan Paul

London, Melbourne and Henley

First published 1961
by Routledge & Kegan Paul Ltd.
39, Store Street,
London, WC1E 7DD,
296, Beaconsfield Parade,
Middle Park, Melbourne,
3206, Australia and
Broadway House,
Newtown Road,
Henley-on-Thames,
Oxon, RG9 1EN
Reprinted 1970
Reprinted in a reduced format
and first published as a paperback 1975
Reprinted 1982
Printed in Great Britain by
Redwood Burn Limited, Trowbridge, Wiltshire
© *Bollingen Foundation 1960*
ISBN 0 7100 6661 9 (c)
ISBN 0 7100 8214 2 (p)

Contents

Translator's Note

This translation has been read and criticized by the author. I am also indebted to my daughter Ximena de Angulo for a rigorous critique of the manuscript. Errors that remain are my responsibility.

CARY F. BAYNES

Morris, Connecticut, Spring 1960

Preface

This little volume consists of lectures given in Peking in the winter of 1943. This was the grim time when the war in China had been going on for almost six years and Peking was under Japanese occupation, a time when all creative forces seemed frozen and darkness ruled the day. During that period there was a group of German-speaking people in the city who kept apart from the activities of the German community and everything connected with it. This group found a center in the home of Wilhelm Haas. Wilhelm Haas is a man with the courage of perseverance; even in the most hopeless situations he has never yielded to despair. And thus it was not by chance that one day he suggested to me that I give some lectures at his house on the Book of Changes. Hesitantly, and only with reluctance, I acceded to his suggestion. This book, its language and imagery, was completely unfamiliar to the audience; moreover, there was at that time a tendency to evade the hardships of the day by dabbling in the occult, and this was a trend I did not wish to encourage. Wilhelm Haas was able to convince me, however, and so I risked the experiment.

The *I Ching*, or Book of Changes, also called the *Chou I*, owes the authority it has always enjoyed in China to a number of causes. One, undoubtedly, is the fact that it has become the first among the Chinese classics. After the Confucian school took up the book in the last period of the Chou era, it became one of the texts whose study was authorized by the government; and when all the non-Confucian schools were excluded from the imperial academy in 140 B.C., the *I Ching* shared with the other Confucian classics in the monopoly of established doctrine. At that time chairs of study were created at the academy for this book, as for the other classics, and this tradition has continued throughout Chinese history. Thus the place of the Book of Changes in Chinese culture rests, in the last analysis, on an act of imperial will. It may occasion surprise that the decree of a temporal power sufficed to give the classics a position that can be compared in other cultures to the place of sacred scriptures inspired by divine revelation. The reason seems to lie in the concentration of divine as well as temporal power in the person of the emperor, in China as well as in other oriental societies. The emperor was not only the sole source of political decisions, he was also the Son of Heaven, the representative of the deity among men; he alone could enact the sacred rites of the great sacrifices, and his decisions consequently had a quality of irrefutability not peculiar to temporal power in the West.

With respect to the *I Ching* there would seem to be, over and beyond the sufficiency of imperial power, reasons why the decree was universally accepted. In the framework of Confucian thought, we must remember, education was not an end in itself. A man was educated for public service, and in a system of increasingly rigid institutions, this meant service as a public official. Now, as an official, an educated man was indeed defenceless vis-à-vis the emperor, and the imperial will was to him an ineluctable fate. The emperors often played their role of fate-makers with a remarkable lack of restraint, and a great number of the educated came to experience this in jeopardy of life and limb. Under such circumstances, the Book of Changes offered a means wherewith a man confronted with imperial whim could still mold his own fate. To the persons in public service, the existing institutions and the position of the emperor were the given conditions of their lives, and indeed the Book of Changes took these conditions into account; within the system, however, the counsels of the book enabled such persons to remain masters of their fates. Furthermore, the concept of change on which the book is based again and again counteracted a tendency toward permanent ossification of the institutions. During the entire course of China's history, her great reformers almost without exception have drawn their inspiration from this book. Since it was a classic, they found in it authoritative backing which helped to smooth the path for their reforms.

In addition to these causalities in the world of Later Heaven, the predominant place of the *I Ching* not only among the educated but among the whole people is due to its character, which differentiates it from the remaining classics. Confucius, despite all his fire, was a person of considerable reserve. His religion was to him a purely personal concern, and not the subject of sermons. What lay beyond the threshold and what motivated his own actions so immediately were things of which he seldom spoke. In later Confucianism, this personal attitude became a trend that gave the whole movement an almost agnostic and certainly a distinctly secular cast. The mission in this world which Confucianism had taken upon itself seemed indeed to require such an attitude. By contrast, the Book of Changes represented the gate to the *whole* man and to the *whole* world, and this complement was as necessary to the emperor and to the official as it was necessary to the subject people, for whom not only the will of the emperor but also that of the official was a component of destiny.

And so it was that until very recently the Chinese turned to the Book of Changes whenever problems arose in the conduct of life. At temple fairs and at the weekly markets were special stalls where one could obtain oracles. At street corners, soothsayers skilled in the oracle had their permanent tables and gave counsel on how to recover a strayed dog or how to deal with a domineering mother-in-law. And at night in the cities, the flute song of blind fortunetellers was to be heard; called into the house, they would feel the signs on the coins with delicate finger tips and would bring forth the wisdom and counsel of the book from the treasure house of memory.

The central position of the *I Ching* is also reflected in the Chinese literature on the subject. In 1692, a bibliography of works on the Chinese classics was published, which contains approximately two thousand titles on the Book of Changes. Some of this material is discussed in the seventh and eighth lectures of this volume. Nor has the tradition been interrupted; up to our own day Chinese scholars have written much, at times perceptively, on questions connected with the book. During the last generation especially, interest grew particularly strong. Western Sinologues, too, have devoted a great deal of attention to it: among the earliest investigators, the Jesuit missionaries at the court of Peking during the seventeenth century. Since then, seven different translations, in Latin, French, and English, have appeared,* and the scholarly journals of the last twenty years have repeatedly published discussions of questions arising out of the texts of the book. In the light of all this, my father's primary object in his translation was to reproduce the *living* tradition of the book and its contents. His close relations with Chinese scholars and men of affairs to whom this tradition was still of personal concern made his task easier.

The lectures reprinted here are based throughout on the work of my father. The texts quoted from the *I Ching* are given in his version. Only very occasionally, where recent research has led to results not yet available to my father, have I deviated from his translation; and in my interpretation I, too, have frequently based myself on the Chinese literature. The present edition reprints the lectures unchanged, in the form in which they were set down at the time.

HELLMUT WILHELM

Seattle, Spring 1958

---

*[In addition to the German translation of Richard Wilhelm: *I Ging, Das Buch der Wandlungen* (Jena, 1924; latest edn., Düsseldorf, 1956). Translated by Cary F. Baynes: *The I Ching, or Book of Changes* (New York [Bollingen Series XIX] and London, 1950), 2 vols. This translation is cited in the present work by bracketed references to volume and page. Minor variations in wording are not noted.]

CHANGE

Eight Lectures on the *I Ching*

1

Origins

Our object is to spend some hours together discussing the Book of Changes. Of course, such an undertaking is not without hazards. This book is difficult to understand; it is so full of cryptic sayings and seemingly abstruse matters that an explanation is often not readily available, and we are tempted to fall back on interpretation to get at the meaning. To us children of an essentially rational generation it poses a problem we are at first reluctant to face; we are led into a region in which we do not know the terrain, and which we have forbidden ourselves to enter except possibly in rare moments of imaginative daring. We ask ourselves if what we are to meet there is not a kind of speculation that lacks any connection with our world. Worse, are we perhaps entering that twilight realm which seduces our generation away from meeting its tasks in the here and now? It is no accident that, of the early Jesuit scholars who were pioneers in making China's culture known in Europe, those who concerned themselves with the Book of Changes were all later declared to be insane or heretic. Indeed, to the Chinese themselves the study of the *I Ching* is not a thing to be undertaken lightly. By an unwritten law, only those advanced in years regard themselves as ready to learn from it. Confucius is said to have been seventy years old when he first took up the Book of Changes.

If nonetheless we undertake to devote some hours to this book, it is because we have important reasons. A book that has stood in such high repute among the men who have determined the fate of China, and that, beginning with Leibniz (we shall have more to say on this point later), has had so much influence on the leading minds of Europe, will have something to offer us also. If we can obtain from it some insight into the minds of our hosts in this country whose guests we are, that in itself will be rewarding. And if, moreover, we should succeed in deriving from it not only understanding, but also genuine illumination, our undertaking will have been entirely justified. We shall do well, though, to keep our doubts in mind as we proceed, rather than suppress them. So may we avoid overenthusiasm and its resulting undertow.

Let us first glance at the appearance and composition of the Book of Changes, in order to get a summary view of the material we are to discuss. The book is based on sixty-four hexagrams, that is, sixty-four six-line figures, each figure or complex being composed of undivided and of divided lines. These hexagrams form the point of departure for what the book has to say. Later we shall deal in detail with the meaning of these lines and with the way in which they are grouped. In the hexagrams, situations are symbolized; they are characterized by the appended names, and these names already take us into the sphere of the book. We find images representing the primary needs of man—for instance, The Corners of the Mouth, symbolizing nourishment—and also images that picture the evolution of personality: Youthful Folly, Molting, Biting Through, Possession, Return (The Turning Point), The Obstacle, Oppression, Standstill, Waiting, Decrease, Retreat; then Break-Through, Pushing Upward, Development, Increase, Abundance, and (the two last images) After Completion and Before Completion. Then there are situations taken from social life: The Marrying Maiden, The Clan, The Well, Fellowship with Men, Holding Together, Approach, Wooing, Coming to Meet, Following, The Power of the Great, Peace; but also Opposition and Conflict. Further, individual character traits are singled out: Modesty, Grace, Innocence, Enthusiasm, Inner Truth. Finally, we find images of suprapersonal significance: The Clinging, The Arousing, Holding Still, The Gentle, The Joyous, and, above all (the first two hexagrams), The Creative and The Receptive.

The linear complexes with their appended titles provide the framework of the subject matter discussed in the Book of Changes. Various categories of Texts elaborate the material in detail. In each hexagram we find at the beginning a brief text, often rhymed, called *T'uan*, a word that originally meant "pig's head" and has been tentatively translated "judgment" or "decision." This judgment sums up the situation, what one may expect of it, and what its chief attributes are.

A second text of more recent date is called *Hsiang*,* "image." This starts from the symbolic meaning of the linear complexes and indicates their basic application to a human, social, or cosmic situation. These image texts, also concise and brief, often have a remarkable beauty of expression. We frequently find in them references to historical situations, or to typical actions and attitudes of compelling symbolic force, and which therefore arouse a desire to emulate. For example, in hexagram 36, Darkening of the Light, it is said:

> The light has sunk into the earth:
> The image of Darkening of the Light.
> Thus does the superior man live with the great mass:
> He veils his light, yet still shines. [I, 150]

In hexagram 28, Preponderance of the Great, the image reads:

> The lake rises above the trees:
> The image of Preponderance of the Great.
> Thus the superior man, when he stands alone,
> Is unconcerned,
> And if he has to renounce the world,
> He is undaunted. [I, 119]

[*Part of the Third and Fourth Wing. See p. 66.—TRANS.]

In hexagram 52, Keeping Still, we have:

Mountains standing close together:
The image of Keeping Still.
Thus the superior man
Does not permit his thoughts
To go beyond his situation. [1, 215]

A third text, *Yao*, adds words to each of the six lines of a hexagram, counting the lowest line as the first and going upward. This group of texts is charged with images and symbols; their immediate relevance to the situation is often hard to see, and at first we must simply accept them as they are, bearing in mind that in the course of our study an explanation may emerge. It is said, for example, that one is:

Wrapped in the hide of a yellow cow. [1, 203]

Or it is said:

The wild goose gradually draws near the shore.
The younger son is in danger.
There is talk. No blame. [1, 219]

Or,

A crane calling in the shade.
Its young answers it.
I have a good goblet.
I will share it with you. [1, 252]

Or,

Someone does indeed increase him.
Ten pairs of tortoises cannot oppose it.
Supreme good fortune. [1, 172]

Or,

One sees the wagon dragged back,
The oxen halted,
The man's hair and nose cut off.
Not a good beginning, but a good end. [1, 159]

These texts, six for each hexagram, often have a common leitmotif that runs through all six lines. Often this is taken from the name of the hexagram, but often too, a metaphor is introduced and different aspects or stages of it are appended to the individual lines. To these three categories of texts, which are regarded as the basic parts of the book, still other material has been added. First, for each hexagram there is a commentary on the *t'uan* text, or the judgment, which is known as the Commentary on the Decision (*T'uan Chuan*) and often gives the reason for the choice of the words in the *t'uan*; and often there is an exposition and elucidation of the attributes of the hexagram.

Another text complex is regarded as a commentary on the words appended to the individual lines. It is made up of brief, often rhymed mnemonic verses that have a connection with the imagery of the line texts.

Still another important text complex is the *Wên Yen*, or Commentary on the Words of the Text. This seems to be a very early commentary, or rather collection of commentaries, of which only fragments concerning the first two hexagrams are extant.

Then there follow two collections of texts, one of which explains the sequence of the hexagrams, giving in many instances interpretations of their names, while the other gives a brief definition of each hexagram as a whole, often drawing a contrast between two of them.

Together with these five texts that can be divided up and allocated to the individual hexagrams, two essays representing a sort of introduction to the work have been incorporated in the book. They are, first, the *Shuo Kua*, Discussion of the Trigrams [1, 281], which interprets the two primary trigrams making up each hexagram, and the symbolic values represented; and second, the so-called Great Treatise, known also under the name *Hsi T'zu*, or Appended Judgments [1, 301], which gives a general introduction to the text of the book as a whole. Further on, we shall discuss this commentary in more detail.

As to the purpose of the *I Ching* and the kind of environment that gave rise to it, these are questions to which a simple answer is not easy to find. It is certain that it was regarded as an oracle book and used as such at a very early date. If, as a starting point, we stick to this fact, something can be deduced about the nature of the soil in which the book grew.

The mental attitude which leads a person to consult an oracle, is, after all, not foreign to our own culture either. We too, are familiar with sybils, prophets, and places from which prophetic sayings emanated.

Such places and institutions owe their existence to the desire for greater understanding inherent in every aspiring individual. To be aware of the situation in which he finds himself and of the consequences that may grow out of it must be the aim of every person who wants to guide his life rather than merely drift with the current. Search for this knowledge by way of oracles has occurred at all times and everywhere, and even today has not wholly died out. Modern psychology has shown us the substructures of the human psyche, which are the source of our strivings to see meaning and order in what is apparently coincidental. Out of this grows our conscious attempt to fit ourselves into the content of this order, so that, in the parallelism between what is without and what is within us, the position and course of the one may also be meaningful for the other. This attitude is old; indeed, it is inherent in human nature. The continents and eras differ only as regards the place where this dark door is sought. Vapors arising from the earth and the stars in their courses have been enlisted again and again as means of obtaining the much sought-for knowledge. In addition, clues that should give the key to this parallelism have been sought in the forces of organic life, especially animal life. Animal oracles of various kinds have existed everywhere. In China, the bone oracle was extensively used from the earliest times.

In contrast to these and even more mechanical efforts, it is important to point out that the oracle of the Book of Changes uses as its key the forces of vegetable rather than animal life. It was a plant growing in sacred places, the yarrow, whose stalks gave access to the oracle when manipulated in a certain way. Clearly, this distinction between the vegetable and the animal indicates not only a difference in method but also a difference in the nature of the oracle.

Another thing that distinguishes the oracle system of the Book of Changes from other similar phenomena is the circumstance that it makes the questioner independent of the mediumistic gifts, or intuition, of an oracle giver. Thus all sorts of influences to which an oracle priest may be exposed were eliminated. It was not a human medium that was consulted but a collection of texts whose authority and value the oracle seeker accepted unquestioningly. For these texts represented to him a fully rounded system, an ordered framework, within which a point to be established would give his momentary situation and what it implied. This system was created by men of ancient times, whom the questioner revered as custodians of a wisdom full of awareness of the connection between what is decreed and what happens. It was from them that he drew his information. This means that the oracle was not born overnight, but must have been preceded by a coherent idea of the cosmos, a definite system of the images of life, that is, a picture of the world, which was then laid down in the Book of Changes.

This brings us to the thing that makes the Book of Changes interesting to persons other than those consulting the oracle. Even if we shrink from approaching the book with the willing faith of an oracle seeker, we can still meditate on this image of the cosmos for its own sake and seek to understand it. The history of the book's origins shows us what can be gained from these reflections.

From what we know of its origins, we cannot say with certainty whether the logical precedence taken by the book and its philosophy over its oracle system corresponds to a precedence in time also; that is, whether the Book of Changes and its picture of the world antedated oracle-taking and, as many persons still think today, did not originally serve the oracle system.

We have seen that the material out of which the book has been composed is heterogeneous throughout, that it does not stem from one period, much less from one man. Chinese tradition concerning its sources, disputed by modern research in every point with more or less reason, places the origin of the different parts in different eras. Tradition says that the legendary culture hero Fu Hsi first devised the linear complexes of the book. Fu Hsi is usually represented as a mountain out of which a leaf-crowned human head emerges. Though this ascription does indeed seem legendary, it is certain at least that the fundamental idea of complexes of whole and divided lines goes back to remote antiquity. Then we are told that the present book has resulted from the revision of two earlier books, also based on the hexagrams, but differing from the present book in the arrangement and names of the individual hexagrams. Of these two books almost nothing trustworthy is preserved to us today except the titles. The first was called *Lien Shan*, "Mountains Standing Together," and is placed in the Hsia dynasty (2205–1766 B.C., traditionally); the later book had the name *Kuei Ts'ang*, "Reverting to the Hidden," and was in use in the Shang era (1766–1150 B.C.). The fact that the Hsia book began with the hexagram for mountain and the Shang book with that for the earth agrees with what we know of the religious beliefs of those times. But these two books contained little of importance besides the linear complexes and their names. A few cryptic sayings of uncertain authenticity that have come down to us in connection with the books tell us but little today. Obviously, various accretions to the saga occurred, if not in writing then in an oral tradition, and these were made use of in the later version. Modern Chinese research has shown that historical allusions harking back to the Shang period are to be found in our texts, indicating that this material of this book must have begun to crystallize in that early time.

The composition of the present Book of Changes, henceforth named *I Ching* or *Chou I*, is attributed to King Wên, father of the founder of the Chou dynasty (1150–249 B.C.), the name of which has been identified with the book ever since. He is said to have established the present arrangement and to have added the *T'uan* texts (Judgments). It is recounted that he completed this work at a time when the last Shang ruler held him captive in his capital. There is nothing in itself improbable in this tradition. Modern Chinese research, which for a long time held widely divergent views as to the time of origin of the *I Ching*, has now come back to placing this stratum of text in the time of King Wên. The reversal of the positions of the first two hexagrams, giving the father predominance over the mother, clearly carries the imprint of the patriarchal Chou dynasty. And whatever else we know about the man Wên, who is honored as a culture hero, does indeed bear out the notion that he occupied himself with the *I Ching*. It is possible, of course, that our present text does not transmit the exact words of King Wên. This reservation applies especially to the auguries "good fortune," "misfortune," "remorse," "humiliation," and so on, which are often appended to the judgments. These terms are so very reminiscent of the tortoise oracle, with which the Book of Changes is otherwise not connected, that we are more or less forced to believe them to be additions made by later adepts in divination who were still familiar with the technique of the tortoise oracle.

These additions probably stem from the same period as the third stratum of text, the *Yao*, or explanations of the individual lines. Tradition has it that these originated with King Wên's son Tan, Duke of Chou, the man who, after the death of his brother, King Wu, carried out the regency for his nephew, Ch'êng in so exemplary a fashion. It is questionable whether Tan's authorship can be validated, but it is certain that this textual stratum also belongs to the early Chou period. In writings of the pre-Confucian period we find it cited along with other oracle books that are no longer extant. If we recognize in whose hands divination rested in the early Chou period, it will be easy to show in what circle the editors of these texts are to be sought. We know that Chou society, in which the use of oracles probably had no place originally, was in the habit of employing a class of the Shang people—a class that had fulfilled like functions in the time of their own dynasty—for divination and related professions. These persons may have filled out the compendium of the *I Ching* by adding the texts to the individual lines. It may be assumed that, in doing this, they made use of the oral traditions connected with the book. Allusions that go back to the early period of the

Chou have also been incorporated. Furthermore, one often has the impression that elements of living folklore, such as farmers' sayings and forecasts, were taken into the book. Naturally, it is quite possible that all of this happened under the direction of the Chou court, which wished to see the work of its ancestors completed, and thus the tradition crediting Duke Tan with this stratum of text might, after all, have a certain validity.

The whole group of additional texts, known collectively under the name "Wings," is ascribed by tradition to Confucius. But this summary ascription cannot be left unchallenged today. It can no longer be said with certainty whether any of the material—and if any, how much—comes from Confucius' own hand. Much of it undoubtedly does come from a source close to him; other parts are clearly stamped as the work of later disciples.

We know that Confucius did occupy himself intensively with the *I Ching*, for even in the remnants of his conversation that have come down to us, we find it mentioned several times. The most plausible assumption is that he discussed this book with his disciples, just as he did other classics, and told them his thoughts about it. Then disciples of a later generation must have gathered these opinions together as commentaries or introductory chapters. In particular, the school of disciples deriving from Tzǔ Hsia appears to have occupied itself with the *I Ching*. He and his pupil K'an-pi Tzǔ-kung may be responsible for many of the present formulations. And it is altogether possible that the older texts also received their final form from these men.

We see, then, that about a thousand years have gone into the making of this remarkable book. Its beginnings go back to times when a rational separation of objective from subjective nature did not yet exist. Those who have collaborated in making it are the personalities who have formed China and its culture. It was completed in the epoch that brought Chinese philosophy to maturity.

2

The Concept of Change

If we turn now to the concept of change which has given the *I Ching* its name and which determines its system of thought, we are immediately reminded of the aphorism *panta rhei*, "everything flows," used by Heraclitus of Ephesus around the year 500 B.C. as the foundation of his own philosophical system. This was about the time when the *I Ching* also took shape, and we have here one of those remarkable instances of parallelism when phases in the development of East and West simultaneously find expression in similar ways. Even this instance, however, so striking at first, discloses on closer examination the typical differences between the two worlds. Heraclitus, who held that life was movement and that it developed through the conflict of opposites, also conceived a harmonious world order, the Logos, that shapes this chaos. But to the Chinese, as we shall see, the two principles, movement and the unchanging law governing it, are one; they know neither kernel nor husk —heart and mind function together undivided.

We have anticipated here; a study of the word which expresses this concept will show us what is meant. The character *I*, which in translation we have simplified as "change," belongs to the original stock of the Chinese language. It is often found on oracle bones and early bronze inscriptions. To throw light on the semantics of this word is not easy, for the most divergent explanations exist. Etymologically, form-parallelism seems to have led to the blending of two different complexes in this word. The first meaning seems to have been "lizard."* This is indicated both by the archaic pictogram, showing a round head, a sinuous body, and an indeterminate number of legs, and by a semantic explanation in one of the oldest dictionaries; the word has retained this meaning, though in later times the classifier for reptile has been added for clearer differentiation. When we stop to reflect that such pictograms were also used to indicate the characteristics of the thing pictured, we come to the concept of easy mobility and changeableness which became associated with this word. For us too, one of the lizards, the chameleon, is the epitome of changeableness.

Then the word must have acquired additional meanings from another Chinese character of similar appearance with which it later became fused. This character, originally meaning "command," was first a pictogram, to which was later added the symbol of power to command, that is, a banner or, originally, an animal's tail. The ideas associated with this word probably included that of a fixed relationship between above and below. In the early bronze inscriptions we also find it meaning the reward granted a vassal by his superior. The word *I* still preserves this meaning, though with the addition of the classifier for gold or metal.

Another explanation finds in the character a combination of sun and moon, that is, of the two fundamental forces, yang and yin, but it is easy to see that this explanation is based on concepts belonging to the *I Ching* itself, and hence it is not of much use in clarifying the evolution of the word prior to the book.

Fusion of the two characters mentioned has given the word *I* the meanings it carries again and again in the ancient writings and which it retains today: the easy, the simple, in contrast to what is difficult; the firm and quiet in contrast to what is endangered; change or alternation.

---

*In the light of recent research this interpretation has come to seem dubious to me. Cf. my "The Concept of Time in the Book of Changes," *Man and Time* (Papers from the Eranos Yearbooks 3; New York and London, 1957), p. 212, n. 2.

In the older strata of the *I Ching*, the word occurs four times. Once it definitely means change, a second time it probably means firm, and the other two times it appears to be a place name, thus complicating things somewhat.

This word *I*, then, has given the name to the book which was arranged and enlarged from existing materials by King Wên at the end of the Shang period, about 1150 B.C. The material he found to hand did not yet bear the name *I*; the new arrangement devised by him was the first to be given this name. We have become accustomed to calling the book the *I Ching*, but *ching* is not an old word; it came into use through parallelism with other texts of the Confucian canon, the Book of History, *Shu Ching*, and the Book of Odes, *Shih Ching*. This designation *Ching* for the classic texts did not come into use until the fourth century B.C., when we first find it used by Chuang Tzŭ. The word actually means the warp of a fabric, and it was probably applied to the classics to differentiate them from the apocrypha, called *wei*, "woof." The old name of the book was *I*, or *Chou I*, Chou being the name of the dynasty whose founders contributed so much to its making. But how the word *I* in this title is to be translated is still a matter of dispute among scholars. Recently it was suggested that the name signifies the easy way (that is, of consulting the oracle), namely that of the Chou, in contrast to the more difficult one of the Shang, using tortoise shells. This and a number of other explanations are unsatisfactory and seem to cover neither the historical nor the intellectual facts of the case. I suggest that we continue to use the name "Book of Changes"; its justification will become apparent in the course of our study. We must bear in mind, though, that the other meanings of the word *I* are always present as undertones. An early apocryphon to the *I Ching* explains this very clearly:

> The name *I* has three meanings. These are the easy, the changing, and the constant. Its character is the easy. Its radiance penetrates the four quarters; simply and easily it establishes distinctions; through it heaven has its brightness. Sun and moon, stars, and regions of the

zodiac are distributed and arranged according to it. The soul which permeates it has no gate, the spirit which it shelters has no entrance. Without effort and without taking thought, simple and without error: this is the easy. Its power is change. If heaven and earth did not change, this power could penetrate nowhere. The reciprocal influences of the five elements would come to a standstill and the alternations of the four seasons would cease. Prince and minister would lose their insignia, and all distinctions would be shifted; what should decrease would grow; what should rule would fall. This is change. Its state is constant. That heaven is above and the earth below, that the lord faces south and the vassal faces north, that the father is seated and the son bows before him: this is the constant. *

These three meanings of the word *I*, which we recognize as the three co-ordinates, here slightly embellished, determining the course of the world, are naturally not to be found so clearly defined in the early strata of the *I Ching*. The later strata then begin to distill the content from the word meanings, and we, too, shall try to make these word meanings our guides to the system underlying the Book of Changes.

The first thing the literal meaning of the character *I* yields us is the easy, the simple, the naturally given. I would like to emphasize this point because it highlights the difference between the system of the Book of Changes in the version presented by the early Chou rulers and in preceding versions. We miss the meaning of this system if at the outset we look for something dark and mysterious in it. The book starts from what everyone sees and can immediately grasp.

That this is true can readily be seen from the historical circumstances out of which the system in its new form arose. The totemistic matriarchal religion of the Shang, which controlled its believers through fear, was alien to the early Chou rulers. Equally alien was that indefinable twilight which permits the sway of the dark forces of the human psyche and provides them with a sanctioned outlet in blood sacrifice. The spirit

---

Chou I Ch'ien-tso-tu.

of the Chou rulers mirrors the simpler and clearer image created by association with vegetative life, that is, with agriculture; their conceptions are not primitive, as one might expect, but have undergone a refining process. In the hierarchy of the instincts, reason—the instinct of the heart, as the Chinese call it—takes over the leadership. Thus the dark force is relegated to the place where it belongs, and it can no longer lay false claim to supremacy. I have, of course, simplified this picture in order to bring out the contrasts. But these spiritual tendencies of the early Chou are also expressed in their social and political systems. Life takes its form from what is given by nature; hence its order is one that can be known, and gods and demons, sinister phantasms that could introduce an irrational element into life, are discredited. This is the special significance of the strict prohibition of alcohol by the early Chou.

The situations depicted in the Book of Changes are the primary data of life—what happens to everybody every day, and what is simple and easy to understand. This point is made very clear in the later strata of the book, which not only aim to present and develop the older system further, but also, in accordance with the social and cultural mission of Confucianism, to demonstrate its efficacy. Again and again the emphasis is on simplicity and lucidity as the only gateway to this system. "The good that lies in the easy and the simple," we read, "makes it correspond to the highest kind of existence." [I, 325] And in another place it is said:

> The Creative knows through the easy.
> The Receptive can do things through the simple.
>
> What is easy, is easy to know; what is simple, is easy to follow. He who is easy to know attains fealty. He who is easy to follow attains works. He who possesses attachment can endure for long; he who possesses works can become great. To endure is the disposition of the sage; greatness is the field of action of the sage. [I, 307f]

Through this gateway we now enter the true province of the Changes. Reflection on the simple fundamental facts of our experience brings immediate recognition of constant change. To the unsophisticated mind, the characteristic thing about phenomena is their dynamism. It is only abstract thinking that takes them out of their dynamic continuity and isolates them as static units. If we seek the parallel to this aspect of change among the concepts of our Western thought, it might be the application of the category of time to phenomena. Within this category everything is indeed in a state of transformation. In each moment the future becomes present and the present past.

The Chinese concept of change fills this category of time with content. It has been formed by the observation of natural events: the course of the sun and stars, the passing of the clouds, the flow of water, the alternation of day and night, the succession of the seasons. And of Confucius also, it is told that, standing by a river one day, he exclaimed: "Like this river, everything is flowing on ceaselessly, day and night" (*Lun Yü*, IX, 16). The concept was formed especially from the pro-creativeness of life. Change is "the begetter of all begetting," [1, 322] it is said, the overflowing abundance of the force which perpetually renews itself and for which there is never standstill nor cessation. It is in constant change and growth alone that life can be grasped at all. If it is interrupted, the result is not death, which is really only an aspect of life, but life's reversal, its perversion.

This perception is highly characteristic of the Chinese concept of change. The opposite of change is neither rest nor standstill, for these are aspects of change. The idea that the opposite of change is regression, and not cessation of movement, brings out clearly the contrast with our category of time. The opposite of change in Chinese thought is growth of what ought to decrease, the downfall of what ought to rule. Change, then, is not simply movement as such, for its opposite is also movement. The state of absolute immobility is such an abstraction that the Chinese, or at least the Chinese of the period which produced this book, could not conceive it. Change is natural movement rather, development that can only reverse itself by going against nature.

The important step carried out in the Book of Changes is the application of this concept of change to the organic forms of life as well. And with this step the book becomes valuable in the philosophical sense;

the insight that man and the natural social groups—that, indeed, the era—can only manifest themselves in this category of change justifies the high expectation with which we approach the *I Ching*. To recognize that man moves and acts, that he grows and develops, this is not deep insight, but to know that this movement and development takes place in typical forms and that these are governed by the law of change, from which there is no escape, this is the knowledge that has fostered in early Chinese philosophy its gratifying integrity and lucidity.

It is not easy to present in plastic form the development that manifests itself in this way, that is inherent in all phenomena. The concept of change is not an external, normative principle that imprints itself upon phenomena; it is an inner tendency according to which development takes place naturally and spontaneously. Development is not a fate dictated from without to which one must silently submit, but rather a sign showing the direction that decisions take. Again, development is not a moral law that one is constrained to obey; it is rather the guideline from which one can read off events. To stand in the stream of this development is a datum of nature; to recognize it and follow it is responsibility and free choice.

When this idea of change is applied to the evolution of an individual man, of social groups and of the era, a series of makeshift hypotheses we have been accustomed to use in explaining events falls away. The principle implies no distinction between inside and outside, content and form. It is implanted in a man's heart; it is active and discernible. In the same way, it is active in human groupings and in whatever is great in the era. Thus it not only embodies, but carries the "soul" of the group, and the "spirit" of the time. The universality of its power includes all levels in all dimensions; every seed that is planted grows and matures within its scope.

The movement of change thus conceived is never one-dimensional in direction. If we keep to an image, cyclic movement is the best term for it. The later commentary literature has made frequent use of this image, but the rigidity that came about because of it is alien to the book itself. The idea of a movement that returns to its starting point, however, is certainly basic. It may have been derived from the orbits of the heavenly bodies or the course of the seasons. To the old Chinese, death itself meant a return. But in such an interpretation more is implied of the idea of self-containment or wholeness than of recurrence. The notion of progress, which we have incorporated in the idea of cyclic movement by the image of the spiral, is alien to the ancient concept of change. The value judgment contained in our idea does not accord with an image made after nature. And the attempt to exalt the new at the expense of the old, the future at the expense of the past, was alien to Chinese thought. The accent lies solely on the ability to keep within the flow of change. If earlier times have been superior to us in this respect, the fact is recognized without prejudice, and the lesson is drawn that we should feel obliged to do as well as the ancients did.

The fact that the movement returns to its starting point keeps it from dispersing, which movement in one dimension only cannot prevent. The infinite is thus brought within the confines of the finite, where alone it can be of service to man.

Thus we approach the third aspect associated with the concept of *I*: the secure, the constant. Early apocrypha already contain the paradoxical definition: "Change: that is the unchangeable." In the later strata of the Book of Changes we find this sense of the word used as the opposite of the word "danger." Danger is the unknown, the mysterious, from which misfortune can arise just as easily as good fortune. Safety is the clear knowledge of the right stand to be taken, security in the assurance that events are unrolling in the right direction.

The early commentators tended to identify this security, as well as constancy, with social relationships. It was said to mean that the father is seated and the son bows before him. This shows them to have been overzealous champions, under the influence of Hsün Ch'ing, of their own social position. Yet the conception was not without dynamism, and the son who bowed before his father today would himself be a father tomorrow and would receive the homage of his son. Thus these social positions are static and fixed only in their relationship; as points of reference in the stream of events they are indispensable. The differences in rank between related positions is by no means as decisive as the fact that a relationship exists. Its polarity introduces a regulatory principle into the course of change. Obviously the possibilities represented by such positions are numerous, father and son being merely one pattern that stands for many. The extended net of relationships—which, in so far as it concerns the group life of men, is naturally social in character— gives change its stability and constancy. But if we transpose the field of change to the personal or the cosmic field, other relationships capable of becoming the measure of this stability are immediately necessary. Later on we shall discuss more fully the fundamental polarity this is based on.

The Book of Changes envisages stability under still another aspect. In the earlier strata of texts it is implicit, and the later texts discuss it in great detail. In these texts the stability of change is the counterpart of the human virtue of reliability. One can grasp it, hold to it, count upon it. Change is not something that is carried out abruptly and irrationally. It has its fixed course in which the trends of events develop. Just as we confidently count on the sun rising tomorrow and on spring following winter, so we can be sure that the process of becoming is not chaotic but pursues fixed courses. We see that here the concept of change comes very close to the Taoist law of the cosmos, the tao of Lao-tse, the meaning of which is so difficult to convey in another tongue. Indeed, much use is made of the word "tao" in the later strata of the book. Here too, tao is the active power in the universe as a whole as well as in each of its parts. We read:

> The Book of Changes contains the measure of heaven and of earth; therefore it enables us to comprehend the tao of heaven and earth and its order. . . . Since in this way man comes to resemble heaven and earth, he is not in conflict with them. His wisdom embraces all things, and his tao brings order into the whole world; therefore he does not err. . . . In it are included the forms and the scope of everything in the heavens and on the earth, so that nothing escapes it. In it all things everywhere are completed, so that none is missing. Therefore

by means of it we can penetrate the tao of day and night, and so understand it. Therefore the spirit is bound to no one place, nor the Book of Changes to any one form. [1, 315–19]

Finally, tao is also that which gives rise to duality, and this saying reminds one immediately of the *Tao Tê Ching.*

Thus the firm, the constant, for which "tao" is here employed is a necessary attribute of the concept of change, and it also implies the idea of consistency and all-inclusiveness. We see that change is at work in the great as well as in the small, that it can be read in cosmic happenings as well as in the hearts of men. From this comprehensiveness of tao, embracing both macrocosm and microcosm, the Book of Changes derives the idea that man is in the center of events; the individual who is conscious of responsibility is on a par with the cosmic forces of heaven and earth. This is what is meant by the idea that change can be influenced. To be sure, such an influence is only possible by going with the direction of change, not against it. Since every seed attains development in change, it must also be possible to introduce into its flow a seed planted by man. And since knowledge of the laws of change teaches the right way of placing such a seed, a highly effective influence becomes possible. Not only that, but planted seeds can be influenced in their development, and the closer to the time of planting the stronger the influence. To recognize the moment of its germination is to become master of the fate of the seed. Here again there comes to mind a passage in the *Tao Tê Ching* containing a similar thought.

In this point of view, which accords the responsible person an influence on the course of things, change ceases to be an insidious, intangible snare and becomes an organic order corresponding to man's nature. No small role is thus assigned to man. Within set limits he is not merely master of his own fate, he is also in a position to intervene in the course of events considerably beyond his own sphere. But it is his task to recognize these limits and remain within them. And to further this understanding by putting the experience of olden times and its wise men at his disposal, the Book of Changes was written.

3

The Two Fundamental Principles

We have discussed the element of constancy or reliability in the principle of change and have noted the definition: "Change: that is the unchangeable." Into the ceaseless change immediately evident to the senses this constancy introduces a principle of order guaranteeing duration in the ebb and flow of events. When man apprehends this principle, he has abandoned the condition of unreflective identification with nature; reflective consciousness enters upon the scene. To become aware of what is constant in the flux of nature and life is the first step in abstract thinking. The recognition of regularity in the courses of the heavenly bodies and in the succession of the seasons first provides a basis for a systematic ordering of events, and this knowledge makes possible the calendar. Similarly the conception of constancy in change provides the first guarantee of meaningful action. The concept takes man out of subjection to nature and places him in a position of responsibility.

Simultaneously with this concept, a system of relationships comes into the idea of the world. Change is not something absolute, chaotic, and kaleidoscopic; its manifestation is a relative one, something connected with fixed points and given order.

Now, in the idea of the world found in the early strata of the Book of Changes, this concept of constancy in change is evoked by the introduction of polarity. Two antithetical points set the fixed limits for the cycles of change. Making use of European terminology, we might rediscover in this system the introduction of the category of space, which, by its co-ordinates, lends the idea of change the stability it connotes. To the early Chinese, space is always three-dimensional. Together with length and breadth, depth was also recognized from the start. Indeed, in early times, this aspect of space received far more attention than surface extension.

The resulting antithesis of above and below is met not only in the Book of Changes; we also find it in those parts of the Book of History and of the Book of Odes whose tradition goes back beyond the Chou dynasty and especially in the inscriptions on oracle bones and on early bronzes. The antithesis of "above and below," however, implies more than just the definition of their relative places. From the outset a relationship between the two positions is indicated: the relationship of correspondence. Above and below are not isolated powers; they are interrelated, and each influences the other. This is clear from the inscriptions on the oracle bones and from ancient songs that reveal their early origin in the fact that what is below precedes what is above. In these testimonia we often find added to the concepts of above and below a third word which characterizes this interrelatedness. "Above and below stand in harmony," it is said, or "Above and below succeed each other." Thus we have documentary proof that this concept existed in the Shang period, and doubtless it is of still greater antiquity.

This antithesis of above and below has been exemplified by the most varied contents. In keeping with the character of the documents which give us the antithesis in its earliest form, the polarity relationship is often a social one. Above is the ruler, below are the people. We find besides—and we will not go far wrong if we assume that this content is even earlier—a cosmic-religious polarity expressed in this relationship, that is, the antithesis between heaven and earth upon which the social polarity is probably patterned. In this pair of concepts, heaven is usually represented by the word *t'ien*, which is still in use in this sense; however, for earth, the modern *ti* is not used, but the older word *t'u*. Here we enter the sphere of the oldest religious intuitions known to us in China. The concept of heaven in this religious significance is without doubt older than the Shang era. As early as the time of the Hsia, heaven, *t'ien*, meant not solely the firmament; naturally, the word connoted also the creative power of heaven. In our terminology, therefore, this word would contain the oldest Chinese concept of God. To what extent an originally anthropomorphic aspect entered into this concept can no longer be known with respect to the earliest times. It might be inferred from the written character that the attribute of vastness and greatness—that is, omnipresence and omnipotence, or better said, supreme creative power—stood in the foreground. Quite early, however, a personal element must have been connected with this concept. The institution of sacrifice to this power cannot be understood in any other way. Very early indeed, perhaps as early as the Hsia, but at any rate by the time of the early Chou, this personal element was given concrete form: the most remote and most revered ancestor was equated with heaven. This occurred in order not so much to create a personal image of God, but to endow the relationship to this God with all the qualities that grow naturally from reverence for the progenitor and from the idea of the continuity of life. The concept of a father in heaven who is our creator is thus presented very concretely. Nonetheless, the equivalence of the ancestor and of heaven did not signify a personification of God, as is evident from the fact that no images of the deity have been found that date from early China.

Contrasted with the Hsia culture, that of the Shang shows a more complex structure. With the rise of the Shang, many widely divergent conceptions were added to the Chinese idea of the world. The Shang were more firmly tied to totemistic views than were their predecessors. The mother stood closer to them than the father; thus it is no surprise that under the Shang, a different, more anthropomorphic concept of God arose, expressed by the word *ti*, which denotes God as well as the divine ruler. Later, this word entered into the emperor concept, *huang-*

ti, "Divus Augustus." In Shang documents we find the word *ti* used also as the antithesis of earth. But the concept of a nonanthropomorphic heaven was not wholly lost during the Shang time, and the early Chou restored it to honor.

There has been much argument as to the degree of correspondence between these early Chinese concepts of God and those of Christianity. The first Jesuit missionaries, especially, made it their business to reconcile the two concepts as much as possible, because they could then build their mission on the thesis that their work consisted in nothing more than leading the Chinese away from more recent and debased views back to their own original heritage. But they did not succeed in winning many among the Chinese to this standpoint, and in the end Rome also withheld its sanction.

The dispute as to whether we have here an early Chinese monotheism in the Christian sense is an idle one, inasmuch as heaven has never been the sole power to which sacrifices were made. That is to say, as far back as the matter can be traced, the Chinese also revered the earth and at times—during the Shang period—gave it more importance than heaven.

Again, the concept of earth, *t'u,* did not signify only concrete things or matter; from the outset a numinous aspect was included in it. The oldest ideogram meaning earth shows a tumulus, a sacred spot on which sacrifices were offered. Though it is an established fact that, during the Shang era and thereafter down to the present, the power sacrificed to was feminine in character, there is abundant evidence of an earlier conception of the earth as masculine. Though their idea of heaven appears to have been based on views held by their predecessors, the Shang seemingly were the first to match this concept with its antithesis and thus to bring out the polarity between heaven and earth characteristic of the Chinese cosmos.

The numinous potency of the earth, manifested in its productive power, though mysterious and hidden, has left an imprint, in still another ideogram that already occurs in the early antitheses. It is the word *shê*, in which *t'u*, the earth, is combined with the classifier for the divine. This added sign really means revelation. What the earth reveals, namely the power of growth, is her spirit, and that is what is revered at the earth-altar, which then also receives the name *shê*. This character *shê*, the earth-altar, later became one of the insignia of Chinese sovereignty and the symbol of Chinese society. Society (in the sociological sense) is *shê-hui*, the union of those gathered together around the altar, the bond connecting the tillers of the soil, who preside over the fertility of the spirit of the earth.

We see then, that the antithesis and the interrelationship of above and below, heaven and earth, with all the meanings is to be found in the oldest Chinese literature. The polarity of these two concepts is built into the system of the Book of Changes and posits the structure in which an ordering principle is latent. It is impossible to overemphasize the dynamism of this process. Polarity here does not mean rigidity, nor a pole around which the cyclic movement turns, but a "magnetic field" which determines the change, indeed evokes it. Thus we encounter this polarity under yet another aspect in the antithesis between the sexes. The feminine earth is contrasted with the masculine heaven, mother earth with father in heaven. Obviously this antithesis between masculine and feminine is a very old one. It too, is to be found in oracle inscriptions and the other early literature, where its symbolic form is the male and female of the animal world. Originally, the male, as the written characters show, was the earth-animal, the animal as related to the earth, and the female was the animal of change, the animal that could bring about transformation. These meanings, particularly the word for female, played a role in later philosophy—in Lao-tse, for instance.

At a very early date, pairs of specific animals represent the antithesis of the sexes: we meet the antithesis in this form in the Book of Changes also. The symbol of the masculine principle is the dragon, of the feminine, the mare. The pairing of dragon and mare, which seems so extraordinary to us, is to be explained by early mythological ideas. The dragon is not foreign to our own mythology, dragon symbolism having probably developed with us in the same stratum of the human psyche as in China. True to the structure of our culture, however, this animal had a totally different function. The dragon represents the masculine principle to us too, and when we wish to curb his fury we sacrifice virgins to him. With us, there is associated with the dragon a conservative element, a propensity for continued possession; the dragon is the guardian of a treasure. This characteristic seems to be part and parcel of the animal's nature, for in China too we find the dragon now and then occupied in guarding treasure. But we think of its power primarily as rampant fury which like a tempest destroys whatever lies in its path. We call upon St. George or the sun hero, Siegfried, to slay the dragon. In China dragons are not slain; rather their electrical power is kept in the realm in which it can be made useful. Thus the dragon stands for a purifying breakthrough, a liberating thunderstorm; it is the supreme symbol of temporal power assigned to the Son of Heaven. Only a dragon that kicks over the traces—which happens also in China occasionally—is dangerous and needs to be subdued.

Contrasting with the dragon and keeping him under control is the mare. Horses were among the first animals to be tamed; they could be taken into service without restriction, but they kept their natural character and, unlike the dog, have not exchanged it for slavish dependence. The horse, then, is at the same time both useful and natural. And so the docile mare acts as counterpole to the roaming dragon. We find this remarkable relationship, rich in symbolic meaning, again and again in images of great plastic force; for instance, at the court of Ming-huang of T'ang (A.D. 713–55), the emperor on his birthday had dancing mares led out before him as an enticement for the imperial dragons of which he was in such great need.

We encounter the mare in this function in the Book of Changes. However, the ancient symbol has been overlaid by a later stratum of myth, and so, following a characteristic reversal of meaning, we find the masculine principle also symbolized by the stallion and the feminine by the gentle cow. The phoenix symbol, which later always appears as the antithesis of the dragon, is probably of more recent origin; apparently, as will be shown later, the mother, K'un, borrowed this attribute from one of her daughters, Li. [I, xxxi]

These animals are indeed only symbols for the polar tension between the sexes originating in the fundamental antithesis of cosmic forces. Later in the Book of Changes this polar tension finds a more abstract expression in concepts that are farther removed from mythological motifs and that represent the active essence of the two positions. These are the paired concepts Ch'ien and K'un. The two words are not easy to translate, and many authors have simply left them untranslated. Probably "The Creative" and "The Receptive" are the translations that best approximate their meaning, because they make clear the idea of the active and the acted upon contained in these concepts. This relationship between Ch'ien and K'un is fundamental even in the earliest strata of the book. Then in the later strata there is much theorizing about it. For example, in the Great Commentary it is said:

> The Creative and the Receptive are the real secret of the Changes. Inasmuch as the Creative and the Receptive present themselves as complete, the changes between them are also posited. If the Creative and the Receptive were destroyed, there would be nothing by which the changes could be perceived. If there were no more changes to be seen, the effects of the Creative and the Receptive would also gradually cease. [I, 347]

> The Creative is the strongest of all things in the world. The expression of its nature is invariably the easy, in order thus to master the dangerous. The Receptive is the most devoted of all things in the world. The expression of its nature is invariably simple, in order thus to master the obstructive. [I, 379]

With their characteristic co-ordinating habit of thought, the ancient Chinese added still other aspects to these pairs of opposites, to some of which we shall return later. The full scope of the conception, however, is manifested in the opposites of yin and yang. These two concepts also are very old, and their interpretation as polar forces began at an early date, the feminine principle taking precedence at that time over the masculine. But again, many generations have worked on the content of this pair of opposites, and it was only in the last third of the Chou era that the two attained their full meaning.

The two written characters that express these two concepts were not, in their earliest forms, the same as they are today; they lacked the classifier now common to both, meaning "mountain slope." Originally yin had only the character for "cloud" and thus meant "the overshadowing," "the dark." In addition, the idea of life-giving water as a dispenser of nourishment is implicit in the image. The character for yang shows a yak-tail, or a pennant fluttering in the sun. Thus something "gleaming in the light," something bright, was meant. The power of command that raises this banner as the symbol of superiority in rank is also contained in this picture, and this added meaning was not lost later. With the classifier signifying "mountain slope" added, yin means "the dark-shadowed side of the slope," that is the north side of the mountain, while yang is the bright, illuminated side, the south side. In a river valley, yang means the bright north side, yin the shady south side. These uses of the two words, current today, give us a good idea of the relativity of the concepts.

These two concepts with the meaning of "bright" and "dark" are already in existence in the older strata of our book. In the *T'uan Chuan* ("Commentary on the Judgments"), [1, 274] they have acquired their basic symbolic value. Then the later strata make explicit much that was previously contained in them implicitly. Thus it is said in the Great Commentary:

> The Book of Changes contains the measure of heaven and earth; therefore it enables us to comprehend the tao of heaven and earth and its order.

> Looking upward, we contemplate with its help the signs in the heavens; looking down, we examine the lines of the earth. Thus we

come to know the circumstances of the dark and the light. Going back to the beginnings of things and pursuing them to the end, we come to know the lessons of birth and of death. The union of seed and power produces all things; the escape of the soul brings about change. Through this we come to know the conditions of outgoing and returning spirits. [I, 315f]

As that which completes the primal images, it is called the Creative; as that which imitates them, it is called the Receptive. [I, 322]

Heaven and earth determine the scene, and the changes take effect within it. The perfected nature of man, sustaining itself and enduring, is the gateway of tao and of justice. [I, 326]

The Master said: The Creative and the Receptive are indeed the gateway to the Changes. The Creative is the representative of light things and the Receptive of dark things. In that the natures of the dark and the light are joined, the firm and the yielding receive form. Thus do the relationships of heaven and earth take shape, and we enter into relation with the nature of the light of the gods. [I, 369]

Chinese philosophy did not fail to note fruitful images of this sort. Tsou Yen, a man of the third century A.D., derived his own particular conception of the cosmos from them, and many of his ideas have gone into the apocryphal literature on the Book of Changes—not always making our understanding of the original content of the book any easier, be it said. The symbolic form these paired forces assumed in the speculations of later philosophers, who evolved from them a kind of gnostic dualistic cosmogony, will concern us later on.

Let us now turn back from these theoretical discussions to the linear complexes of the Book of Changes. The sixty-four situations dealt with in the book are represented by complexes of six lines each, that is, by sixty-four hexagrams. The individual line carries the polar tension we have been discussing. The tension is expressed by the line, and the situation is defined in a sixfold combination of the bipolar forces. Thus we find in the six places of the hexagram lines of two sorts, a whole, undivided line, representing the yang force, or a line divided in the middle, representing the yin force.

There has been much discussion as to how these line configurations arose, and frequent attempts have been made to show that they are fertility symbols. At all events, this interpretation reflects their meaning only partially. Undoubtedly they possessed a much broader meaning even at the time of their origin. The most plausible explanation is that they are a by-product of the method of consulting the oracle. The oracle's pronouncement was obtained with the help of plant stalks; and it would be natural to use the oracle stalks to represent the answer. Apparently, the elaborate way of consulting the oracle described in the later strata of the book, and still practiced today, was not in use in early times. At first the method seems to have been a sort of drawing of lots, wherein long stalks meant a positive answer and short stalks a negative. Then, because of the equality in rank of the two fundamental forces, and probably also because of the old conception that heaven is one and earth two, two short stalks were made equal to one long stalk and were used to symbolize the yin force.

These two sorts of lines, whole and divided, were given the names "firm" and "yielding." They define yet another exceedingly important aspect of polarity. In the older strata of the book these are the names most frequently given the two fundamental forces. The Great Commentary also makes frequent use of them. It is said there: "The firm and the yielding are images of day and night." [1, 311] And in a more detailed passage we read:

Heaven is high, the earth is low; thus the Creative and the Receptive are determined. In correspondence with this difference between low and high, inferior and superior places are established.

Movement and rest have their definite laws; according to these, firm and yielding lines are differentiated. [1, 301]

Reducing the two fundamental forces to the line configurations of the Book of Changes immediately places these forces within the process of change. They are no longer as abstract and remote as they seemed in our foregoing analysis, for they too are subject to change and thereby produce alteration and transformation.

The holy sages instituted the hexagrams, so that phenomena might be perceived therein. They appended the judgments, in order to indicate good fortune and misfortune.

As the firm and the yielding lines displace one another, change and transformation arise. [I, 309f]

In this way the line configurations give an image of the changes in the phenomenal world, for the firm lines are transformed and become yielding and the yielding lines alter and become firm. Each of the two sorts of lines, then, and the polar opposites for which they stand, have two states of being, one of rest and one of movement, which represent the different aspects of their character.

In a state of rest the Creative is one, and in a state of motion it is straight; therefore it creates that which is great. The Receptive is closed in a state of rest, and in a state of motion it opens; therefore it creates that which is vast. [I, 324]

The firm line thus has unity for its quality and is one-dimensional in direction. It is an image of man's mind. The yielding line shows the vegetative movement of opening and shutting and thus symbolizes man's soul.

The manner in which the development of the individual lines is carried through is decisive for the system of the book. The firm line pushes outward, thus becomes thin in the middle and breaks in two, forming a divided line. The yielding line, on the other hand, pushes inward and thereby finally grows together into an undivided line. Thus in the process of change, these lines transform into their opposites. Therefore, every component of the situation can reverse itself and bring a new element into the situation as a whole—a fundamental truth also familiar to us of the West. Later on, Lao-tse clothed this idea in the saying: "Reversal* is the movement of tao."

Closer study shows that this principle of reversal of qualities also contains a maxim for action, which again appeals to the man who is conscious of responsibility, but which takes us a step further than the mere possibility of conformity in our actions mentioned above. Viewed from this standpoint, our reflections and actions show themselves to be not only possible, but also posited. This has the negative meaning that everything absolute and unconditional already implies its own death. On the other hand, it also means that easy conformity, a habit of allowing oneself to drift this way and that, an unresisting acceptance of developments, sweeps one into the current of events from which escape is no longer possible. Only by taking up a counterposition, by confronting events with live awareness, can developments be guided into the desired paths.

The pattern of events, though, is complicated, and obviously whole and divided lines would not suffice to represent it adequately. We must turn now to the more complex pictures of the situation—the images—and what they imply.

---

*I.e., change from one opposite to the other. [The quotation is from the *Tao Tê Ching*, ch. 40. In the J. J. L. Duyvendak tr. (London, 1954; p. 96): "The movement of the Way is: to reverse."—Tr.]

4

The Trigrams and the Hexagrams

We have tried to sketch the system on which the Book of Changes is based. We saw that the whole order underlying the world and life is imaged in two lines charged with spiritual meaning. These lines are an embodiment of the orbit of change and of the two poles that determine it. It is important to think of this representation as very concrete. Today we tend to speak of "symbols" in such a context, each person varying at will the distance between the symbol and the thing symbolized. In a magical world view, however, such as the one which has left its impress on the oldest strata of our book, a thing and its image are identical. We need not be taken aback because these images have taken on so rational a form as that of a divided and an undivided line instead of being presented more fancifully. The infinite complexities of phenomena have been invested in a rational form accessible to man's intellect and power of action in order to indicate that aspect of phenomena which may lead to insight and action. According to tradition, these linear images were devised by the holy men and sages of long ago, who in turn are the most important agents in the phenomenal world; the linear images completely contain the world, they are its embodiment.

In the late strata of the Book of Changes, the idea of "like" has begun to interpose itself between what was represented and the image representing it. The images are no longer the things themselves, they are only *like* the things. Even the explanations in the Great Commentary, however, still show traces of the old standpoint:

> Therefore, with respect to the Images: The holy sages were able to survey all the confused diversities under heaven. They observed forms and phenomena, and made representations of things and their attributes. These were called the Images. The holy sages were able to survey all the movements under heaven. They contemplated the way in which these movements met and became interrelated, to take their course according to eternal laws. Then they appended judgments, to distinguish between the good fortune and misfortune indicated. These were called the Judgments. The exhaustive presentation of the confused diversities under heaven depends upon the hexagrams. The stimulation of all movements under heaven depends upon the Judgments. [I, 348]

The increasing abstraction of the image from the thing symbolized permits the value of the image to be fully exhausted. It is the step from magical involvement in phenomena to imposing order on them and mastering them. From an attribute of things, the image develops into a means of understanding and mastering them, a means that remains superior to more ephemeral media such as writing and speech.

> The Master said: Writing cannot express words completely. Words cannot express thoughts completely.

> Are we then unable to see the thoughts of the holy sages?

> The Master said: The holy sages set up the images in order to express their thoughts completely; they devised the hexagrams in order to express the true and false completely. Then they appended judgments and so could express their words completely. [I, 346]

Nonetheless, when we come to explaining the situations pictured, we shall do well to keep in mind the original merging of thing and image. Only on this basis does much of the text and much of what is derived from it become intelligible.

The system of linear complexes that make up the hexagrams develops naturally and logically from the imagery of the divided and undivided lines. By adding another line, four configurations of double lines are obtained: the old yang, consisting of two undivided lines ⚌; the young yang, an undivided and a divided line ⚎; the young yin, made up of a divided line and an undivided line ⚍; and finally the old yin, two divided lines ⚏. The lower line, on which the structure is built up, is thus the one which determines the character of the combination. If another line is added to each of these four configurations, we obtain the eight trigrams, and from the superposition of these upon one another, the sixty-four hexagrams result. This is the process which the *Tao Tê Ching* describes in the following words: "Tao gave birth to the one, the one gave birth to the two, the two gave birth to the three, and the three gave birth to all things." *

Whether this logical order corresponds to the historical sequence is an open question. There are many indications that the hexagrams were the original images from which the trigrams were then later abstracted and that the configurations of double lines are derived from a still later analysis. In favor of this hypothesis is the fact that the numbers two and six on which the hexagrams are based have a long history of special emphasis in the numerical system. The number six probably antedates even the Hsia period. In fact, as later speculations again and again show, six seems to be one of the most commonly emphasized numbers in a primitive context, while three and eight seem to have gained attention much later. Then too, it is not easy to accept the simple summing up of one and one and one as having been the way in which the phenomena under heaven were mirrored. The law underlying the formulation of one and one and one is, of course, inherent in things, but the knowledge of it appears to be alien to the original perception of phenomena and would seem to belong to a later systematization. The later rationalization only goes to show how adequate the original vision was.

---

*[*Tao Tê Ching*, ch. 42. Cf. Duyvendak, p. 99.—Tr.]

This brings us to a question posed repeatedly by the Book of Changes: in which stratum does the real meaning of this book lie? Is it in the very oldest store of images and ideas occasionally shining through the strata belonging to the early Chou era and later? Is it in the systematization undertaken in King Wên's time? Is it the inclusion of folk sayings and verses that gives the book its extraordinary depth? Or does it derive from the intellectual and spiritual refinement the book underwent at the hands of the Confucian School in the last third of the Chou era? For even this is not the last stratum. It has been topped by the commentaries and apocryphal literature of the outgoing Chou, Ch'in, and Han eras—fed in part from the schools of magic of popular Taoism—not to mention the later speculative ideas that have become decisive in the exegesis of the book. All these strata are more or less transparent; the old shines through in the new and lives on in it. Some strata can be isolated with relative certainty, but some other features are not at all easy to assign to the right group.

But the essential thing is to keep in mind all the strata that go to make up the book. Archaic wisdom from the dawn of time, detached and systematic reflections of the Confucian school in the Chou era, pithy sayings from the heart of the people, subtle thoughts of the leading minds: all these disparate elements have harmonized to create the structure of the book as we know it. Its real value lies in its comprehensiveness and many-sidedness. This is the aspect under which the book lives and is revered in China, and if we wish to miss nothing important, we must not neglect the later strata either. In these, many of the treasures of the very earliest origins are brought to light, treasures that up till then were hidden in the depths of the book, their existence divined rather than recognized. When the occasion arises, we shall follow the lines leading back from the later to the earlier elements, in the hope that from the study of the living development of the book itself we may also derive insight into its meaning.

Let us first examine the eight trigrams, the line configurations inherent in all of the hexagrams. To begin with, we have the pair of opposites, Ch'ien and K'un, two trigrams that consist of three undivided lines in the one case and of three divided lines in the other, that is to say, of three yang and three yin lines respectively. The names given these trigrams are not easy to decipher; their oldest meaning is probably "the dry" and "the moist," that is to say, the separation of land and water, which with us too stands at the beginning of creation. In China, however, this separation is not one of surfaces, for Ch'ien does not mean the continent, nor K'un the ocean; the accent is on the active force of the elements represented. Thus Ch'ien means what the earth brings forth, and K'un means the thing that nourishes what is brought forth. In these original meanings of the words we come on an extremely early tradition that the earth or at least its product is masculine; later, this conception turned into almost its opposite. The change of meaning undergone by the trigram Ch'ien has never wholly obscured this early phase and the resulting ambivalence enhances its truth to nature and endows it with great energic force.

Even in the early Chou period, however, Ch'ien had already grown beyond the earth completely and had risen above it, while K'un moved partly into the abandoned position. In this period we encounter them as heaven and earth. But these images also are dynamic, the quality of their action being more important than the mode of their being. Heaven is the creative element, the sovereign, the prince and the father. Earth is the receptive principle that adapts itself devotedly to him who stands above it; it is the mother, and the mass ruled from above. Ch'ien is head, K'un the abdominal cavity. Ch'ien is round and expansive, K'un square and flat. Ch'ien is cold and ice, K'un the cloth that warms and the kettle containing nourishment. Ch'ien is the cutting edge of metal; it is smooth jade. K'un is a big wagon that holds and transports things with ease. Ch'ien is energy and K'un is form; and reflecting Ch'ien's earlier meaning, it is the fruit, while K'un is the trunk of the tree. Ch'ien is a strong red and K'un a deep black. Ch'ien is the place where the opposites confront each other. "God battles in the sign of the Creative," it is said; "the dark and the light arouse each other." [I, 287, 289] Indicative of wide experience and keen observation is the fact that this event was assigned to the northwest and its time given as late autumn and early winter, or in diurnal terms, the time just before midnight: the time when the opposites meet, when the decisive battles are fought, as everyone knows who has ever noted the rhythm of his psyche. K'un on the other hand is the scene of peaceful labor. "God causes things to serve one another in the sign of the Receptive," it is said. K'un is the ripening season of late summer; it is the afternoon lit up with warm sunshine.

We have already encountered the animal symbols of these two trigrams. Originally, Ch'ien was the dragon, K'un the mare. Later, the horse in many forms stood for Ch'ien; a thin horse, an old one, and a wild horse is Ch'ien, while the cow—or a calf with a cow—appeared as K'un. This change may also indicate a historical development. The dragon is originally a mythological heritage of the well-watered south where the Tai people especially keep its memory green. But the horse seems to have come from the north. From this dragon-mare antithesis we might deduce the overlaying of a northern culture by a forward push of the south. Cattle, on the other hand, belong to the west, to proto-Tibetan peoples perhaps. A horse culture would seem to have gained the upper hand over an earlier cattle culture. In any event, the fact that the dragon as well as the horse has left an imprint in the trigram Ch'ien once again contributes to its singular dynamic ambivalence.

The remaining six trigrams show a mixture of whole and divided lines. They fall into two groups, the light or masculine trigrams, representing the three sons, and the dark or feminine trigrams, representing the three daughters. It is somewhat surprising at first glance that the light trigrams are those with more dark lines and the dark trigrams those with more light lines, and that the line differing from the other two is the one that determines the complex as a whole. The reason assigned for this is that the light trigrams have an odd-number value and the dark trigrams an even-number value, an idea not unknown to modern psychology.

To explain this sentence we must briefly go into the number symbolism of the lines, which represents an evolution from the original six to the more complex nine. The nine came to the fore at the beginning of the Chou period. A yin line was indicated by six, a yang line by nine, which united within itself a feminine four and a masculine five. But the six and nine are only the two extremes; they show yin and yang at the peak of movement, while in between there are the stages of seven and eight—that is, yang and yin at rest, the odd seven symbolizing yang and the even eight yin. Thus the light trigrams consist in each case of two even lines (six or eight) and an odd line (nine or seven), hence the sum of the symbolical numbers in this case is odd. The dark trigrams, on the other hand, always show two odd lines and one even line, hence they always add up to an even number.

The three light trigrams are Chên, K'an, and Kên. In the first of these the light line is the lowest, in the second the middle line, and in the third the top. The first trigram, Chên ☳, is the eldest son, and its attribute is the Arousing. Its image in nature is thunder. "In the trigram of the Arousing, she [K'un] seeks for the first time the power of the male and receives a son. Therefore the Arousing is called the eldest son." [1, 294] Chên is movement and speed; it is young, green bamboo; it is reeds and cane. It is the strong and rapidly growing son, on whom, as firstborn, the mother's care and the father's concern are expended. It has taken over from the father the symbol of the dragon and among horses those noted for swiftness, for notable markings, or for being outstanding in some other way. Chên is a horse with white hind legs, or with a star on the forehead; it is a neighing, a galloping horse. Among plants, strange to say, pod-bearers are assigned to Chên. Its color is dark yellow; its part of the body is the foot, which serves movement; its field of activity is the road leading to the goal. It means the east, spring, the time of blossoming, of expansion, the beginning of all new things. "All living things come forth in the sign of the Arousing," [1, 288] we are told; it is the time when God reveals himself in thunder.

41

The second trigram is K'an ☵, the Abysmal, the middle son. The Abysmal is water, and particularly the rapid water flowing through a gorge. The second son thus also in a sense resembles his mother more than his father, having absorbed one of her oldest attributes. Because of this ambiguity, the trigram also signifies danger. The other attributes underline this ambiguous character. From water K'an derives its penetrating or piercing characteristics; but it also means the ditch in which one hides oneself and, indeed, even means a thief in hiding. It is blood; its color is blood red. Among men, it is the melancholic, the sick in spirit, the man with earache. Its animal is the pig, its part of the body the ear that listens into the abyss. Among horses, sickly ones are related to K'an, those with hanging heads and those with hooves that are too thin, those that stumble; but on the other hand, those with beautiful backs and with a wild courage also belong to K'an. It is a defective wagon, but also the wheel of the wagon; it is everything bent and bending, the bow, and finally the moon. Be it noted that in this stratum of culture the moon is still masculine. K'an is due north, midwinter, and midnight, the time of toil. Indeed, this last aspect contains the positive side of the trigram. It is said: "God toils in the sign of the Abysmal, and all living creatures are subject to him," [I, 289] that is, endurance in danger and trouble will be crowned with success. This characteristic of perseverance is emphasized by the fact that in the plant world, hard, pithy wood is associated with K'an.

The last of the light trigrams is Kên ☶, Keeping Still, standing fast, the youngest son, whose image is a mountain. It is a narrow mountain path full of small stones, a mountain pass and a gate, and at the same time the watchman at the gate and palace; therefore, among animals, the dog. It has taken over an attribute of the father, fruit, meaning the completion of the plant; and the fruit is likewise the seed out of which the new entity develops. It is a knotty tree, a black-billed bird. The part of the body belonging to Kên is the hand, the fingers. There is no connection with horses in this trigram. Kên stands in the northeast; with respect to the day, it is the turning point when night turns into early morning, when what began as a struggle in the early night is brought to completion. Therefore it is said of it: "God brings all living things to perfection in the sign of Keeping Still." [1, 287]

The three daughters are the trigrams Sun, Li, and Tui, in which the dark line stands first at the bottom, then in the middle, then on top.

The eldest daughter is Sun ☴, the Gentle. Its image is the wind, penetrating everywhere, and from this comes its attribute, penetration; it also stands for the vegetative power in wood. "In the trigram of the Gentle the male seeks for the first time the power of the female and receives a daughter. Therefore the Gentle is called the eldest daughter." [1, 294] It is significant that the mother seeks sons from the father, but the latter seeks daughters from the mother. The Gentle symbolizes straightforward, persevering labor; length and height; the eyes; one whose talents for economy fit her to obtain threefold value in the market-place—that is, she is the one who brings increase to the household. She is the person who quietly weighs and considers, who knows when advance and when retreat is indicated, but this weighing can also indicate indecision. White is her color. Much white in the eyes indicates vehemence, and so in this dual characteristic she stands especially close to the eldest brother. Her vehemence, however, is only an occasional outburst; as a whole, she embodies purity and completeness. "God brings all things to completion in the sign of the Gentle." [1, 287] The symbolic animal assigned to Sun is the cock, a first step toward the phoenix, which later developed from it. The thighs are the portion of the body associated with this trigram. Its position in space is southeast and its time is forenoon, the time of hard work.

Li ☲, the next trigram, carries the image of fire and of the sun. Here we encounter a sun that is feminine. The characteristic of Li is the clinging quality of fire and the brightness of the sun. This brightness can be so intense that it means lightning. Fire also implies dependence on the matter consumed. The part of the body associated with Li is the clear eye, as is natural. From her father this daughter has inherited dryness, and so she can also stand for a withered tree. Transferred to the world of man, fire and lightning are dangerous weapons, and so shield and helm, lance and weapons, are attributes of this Pallas Athene.

Strange to say, she has a large belly, a trait which probably comes from the structure of the trigram, firm and hollow within. The animal symbolizing Li is the pheasant, again a creature close to the phoenix of later times. However, she achieves a quality of tension between the opposites from having tamed a number of water animals: turtle, crab, snail, mussel, and tortoise. Li occupies the south, and her time is summer and bright, scorching midday. This trigram is the scene of perception. "God causes creatures to perceive one another in the sign of the Clinging," [1, 287] it is said, and it is remarked in explanation: "That the holy sages turned their faces to the south while they gave ear to the meaning of the universe, means that in ruling they turned to what is light." [1, 289]

The last of the eight trigrams is Tui ☱, the youngest daughter, who spreads gaiety and joy around her. Her symbol is the quiet lake, and still, deep water. This lake gives back what is mirrored in it, and it is thus reflection. Connected with this resilience is the meaning of dropping down and bursting open. The part of the body associated with Tui is the mouth. This means not only Lucullan pleasures, but also speech. Many strange hidden things can push up from the depths of the lake whose surface lies so quiet. Thus Tui is a sorceress, and the enticing water of the lake can suggest the idea of destruction and ruin. The structure of the trigram indicates hardness, even intractability inside, but outside it is yielding. Thus Tui can be the concubine, and among animals the sheep. The trigram Tui stands in the west; its time is mid autumn and the evening which rejoices all creatures. Therefore it is said: "God gives creatures joy in the sign of the Joyous." [1, 287] But we must not forget that an excess of joy has its dangers. Tui is closest to the youngest brother, the mountain, to whose powers she joins hers.

Approximately, that is the content of the eight trigrams. According to the situation, now one, now another of these various meanings and symbols is in the foreground, but we must bear all of them in mind if we wish to dissect the hexagrams into their component parts.

The hexagrams represent two trigrams placed one above the other; at any rate, they were already viewed this way at the beginning of the Chou era. Thus a combination of trigrams determines the image belonging to the hexagram in question, the image being made up of the meanings and inner dynamism of the two trigrams. For example, a combination of Ch'ien and K'un can take place in two ways. Suppose, first, that Ch'ien is below and K'un above it; this means a particularly close union of the two primal powers, because heaven has the tendency to rise and K'un to sink. They move toward each other. The picture presented by this hexagram is therefore altogether favorable. It is the eleventh hexagram, T'ai, Peace, the beginning of the union and development of all things. But if the combination is the other way round, the picture is nothing like as favorable. The two halves then strive to part and heaven tends to leave the earth behind. The result is the twelfth hexagram, P'i, Standstill, the time in which nothing prospers.

However, this is not the only way in which trigrams are used to explain the hexagrams. While on the one hand, the two half signs constitute lines 1 2 3 and 4 5 6 of a hexagram, on the other hand two other trigrams, called nuclear trigrams, can be formed from lines 2 3 4 and 3 4 5. In the hexagram T'ai, which shows heaven below and earth

above, the two nuclear trigrams are Tui ☱ below and Chên ☳ above. In the opposite hexagram, P'i, Standstill, they are Kên, Keeping Still ☶ below and Sun, the Gentle, the Indecisive ☴ above. Thus the nuclear trigrams contribute to the explanation of the situation as a whole.

A hexagram is studied from below upward, and as a rule, the different lines represent progress in the situation. For example, a situation in itself favorable can also reveal unfavorable aspects at the beginning when it is still embryonic, or at the end when its influence is ebbing.

The top line of the hexagram T'ai, Peace, clearly demonstrates the cessation of such an influence, when order falls again into chaos. The text for this line reads: "The wall falls back into the moat. Use no army now. Make your commands known within your own town. Perseverance brings humiliation." [1, 53] The text for the top line of Standstill says: "The standstill comes to an end. First standstill, then good fortune." [1, 57]

There is an especially favorable correspondence between certain places and certain individual lines. A firm line is correct in the first, third, and fifth places, and a yielding line is correct in the second, fourth, and sixth places. Naturally, the correctness of the position also has a significance. Thus in Standstill, the six in the second place is in a correct position and the text for it contains the words: "[Even] the standstill serves to help the great man to attain success." [1, 56] The nine in the fourth and the nine in the sixth places of this hexagram also are by no means unfavorable lines. A correct position is not always an advantage, however. A firm line in a firm place can mean too much firmness, just as a yielding line in a yielding place occasionally marks the absence of a requisite firmness. But a central position of the line, that is, in the middle of a primary trigram, is favorable as a rule. The fifth is the place of the ruler, the place in which a situation bears full fruit but in which the signs of decadence do not yet manifest themselves. The second is the place of the official in the provinces, who advances himself but little and works on details. The fourth place, near the ruler, is termed the place of the minister. Thus, for example, it is said of the six in the fifth place in hexagram 12, T'ai, Peace: "The sovereign I gives his daughter in marriage. This brings blessing and supreme good fortune." [1, 53] (This daughter became the mother of King Wên.) And about nine in the second place it is said:

Bearing with the uncultured in gentleness,
Fording the river with resolution,
Not neglecting what is distant,
Not regarding one's companions:
Thus one may manage to walk in the middle. [1, 51]

This is to say that even in times of peace, the lot of the official is thorny and full of responsibility.

Some lines stand in a particularly close relation to one another. Thus the first and third, the second and fourth, the third and fifth correspond, particularly when the lines in question differ in character. The correspondence is notably strong between the two central lines and is favorable as a rule where a strong official corresponds to a yielding ruler. The opposite case is nothing like as favorable. Naturally, the relation between ruler and minister, the fifth and fourth lines, is also close. The relation is usually favorable when a strong ruler has an obedient and adaptable minister; a stronger minister all too easily involves a yielding ruler in difficulties. Other neighboring lines can also have relationships, as for instance the two top lines, which then symbolize a ruler who yields to the counsel of a sage.

Apart from these peculiarities of character pertaining to the individual lines and places, each hexagram has its ruler. Of these there are two kinds, the constituting and the governing ruler. The constituting ruler of a hexagram is always that line which expresses most clearly the characteristic feature of a situation. In Standstill, for example, this is the six in the second place, which has the text: "They bear and endure." The governing ruler usually coincides with the ruler's place in the hexagram and is thus, for the most part, represented by the fifth line. Occasionally, however, there are two lines of equal strength, which are then both regarded as governing rulers.

These are the basic features underlying the system of the hexagrams. One's situation in time and the potentialities implied in it can be known through the aid of these hexagrams. The point of this knowledge, though, is solely to provide the right basis for action. Therefore it is said:

> The changes and transformations refer to action. Beneficent deeds have good auguries. Hence the images help us to know the things, and the oracle helps us to know the future. [I, 380]

5

The Hexagrams Ch'ien and K'un

The system of the sixty-four hexagrams by which the extent and configuration of the changing world is plotted as if by landmarks is highly interesting from the outset, for the number and make-up of the individual hexagrams is fixed by mathematical law. Nothing can be added, nothing taken away. Scholars have in fact extended the mathematical order underlying the individual hexagram and, applying it to the system as a whole, have obtained a perfect numerical representation satisfying to the imagination of a mind trained in mathematics. A graphic representation of this system cannot but be inadequate, because three dimensions do not suffice. That is to say, if a single line is delineable in one dimension, and the double line requires a plane, and for the trigram a solid body is necessary (the representation of the eight trigrams at the eight corners of a cube yields a picture of remarkable compactness), then naturally when it comes to representing the complex of a hexagram, one cannot do without the help of a fourth dimension, which is indeed imaginable to the mathematical mind but which cannot be represented concretely.

The mathematically perfect structure of the single hexagrams and the absolutely logical construction of the system as a whole thus yield a strict norm which underlies individual, changing situations and at the same time provides the frame for life in all its comprehensiveness. It is to be noted that this mathematical frame is not a strait jacket; the coincidence of the situations of life with the mathematical intersections provided by the system is by no means arbitrary. This attempt to view the totality of changing phenomena in terms of such a strict law of form may appear strange to us. The fact, however, that nature lends itself more easily to such systematizations than does the human mind is witnessed—to cite one example—by the arrangement, as rigid as it is natural, of the elements in the unbroken order of their atomic numbers. The occasional gaps, it became clear, were to be attributed to the state of chemical research and not to defects in the system. It is the same with the system of the hexagrams and the images represented by them. Ancient Chinese thinkers noted certain co-ordinations, which later observers must accept, just as we have to accept the fact that the atomic number of iron is 26 and that of gold is 79. Closer study will show that these co-ordinations are not arbitrary, and that they get at the essentials of a given situation.

The second thing which a European mind finds difficult to accept are the texts accompanying the individual hexagrams. What can be done with sayings like "pigs and fishes" or "he treads on the tiger's tail"? These too we must simply accept at first, as we accept a musical composition, in which it is not always immediately evident why this or that modulation or harmony stands in this or that place, yet the whole composition carries conviction. To continue the comparison: the structure of the hexagram, and its relation to the system, determine the musical form, so to speak, while the image of the situation furnishes the theme. No absolute limitation is imposed upon the freedom of the musical imagination in developing the theme within the frame of a definite form. But we can enjoy the music only when we follow this imagination; the closest possible union between theme and form further the perfection of the expression in a natural way. A thorough analysis of the texts accompanying the hexagrams will yield us many insights concerning their composition. The fact that in most cases a nonrational element remains that eludes logical analysis must be credited to the creative imagination of the authors of the texts.

The composition of these accompanying texts is not carried out according to a fixed schema. Making the necessary allowances, we can distinguish two fundamental types. The first, clearer, type suggests the musical pattern of theme and variations. The chosen theme persists through the six stages, in various aspects. The second type is more difficult to analyze. A recurrent leitmotiv is lacking here; instead, six different stages whose connection is usually an inner one are joined together in mosaic fashion. But in both types, the so-called judgment is the tenor which is maintained through all the changes.

The two hexagrams Ch'ien and K'un, with which the Book of Changes begins, are the best examples of these two types of composition. In a detailed study of the two hexagrams we shall acquaint ourselves with their range of ideas by examining their formal construction.

The hexagram Ch'ien, first in the book since the beginning of the Chou era, consists solely of undivided lines. Thus all of the trigrams in it, the primary as well as the nuclear, are the trigram Ch'ien. Throughout the book, hexagrams that show a doubling of a primary trigram are given the same name as the trigram. Ch'ien, then, is the unlimited embodiment of the strong, light, active, creative power, whose symbol is heaven. In relation to the world of man it stands for a creative personality in a leading position, the holy ruler. In the rotation of the seasons it is associated with the Chinese fourth month, approximately our May— that is, the time when growth and flowering is at a peak, before the setting in of the opposite movement has made the yin power felt. It is characteristic of the Chinese attitude that the time of the most abundant light does not coincide with the month containing the longest day, but with the month before it: before completion gives birth to the onset of reaction.

As is the case with every hexagram, this image is provided with a commentary deducing definite rules for action from the situation. The text reads:

The movement of heaven is full of power.
Thus the superior man makes himself strong without tiring. [I, 5]

Ch'ien, then, stands for the time of construction, of lasting and unremitting creative work, which can be fulfilled only by single-minded, uncompromising strength. The image of heaven redoubled stands for the recurrent and ceaseless productivity that draws power from itself; it stands for the time of self-fertilizing, many-sided activity.

The Judgment, the *Tuan* text, therefore also consists of favorable phrases signifying the four qualities of heaven in its cyclic movement. First is *yüan*, the sublime beginning; second, *hêng*, i.e. pushing through to success; third, *li*, usefulness that furthers; and last, *chên*, firm perseverance. In these attributes the cycle of creative activity is given. One may also discover in them symbols of the four seasons. However, more important is their co-ordination with cosmic and human activity. In the later strata this is amplified in detail. It is said:

> Great indeed is the sublimity of the Creative, to which all things owe
> their beginning and which permeates all heaven. [II, 2]

Here we see the two first attributes summed up and united in a single concept, "sublime success," and the paired arrangement of the four phrases is retained in later commentaries. The effect of the second pair of phrases "perseverance that furthers" is characterized as follows:

> The clouds pass and the rain does its work, and all individual beings
> flow into their forms. [II, 3]

This is the fertilizing power of heaven, to which beings owe their enduring forms and which determines their nature and kind.

In the Commentary on the Words of the Text (*Wên Yen*), an early commentary preserved for the first two hexagrams only, we find these statements: [I, 8–10]

> Of all that is good, sublimity is supreme. Succeeding is the coming
> together of all that is beautiful. Furtherance is the agreement of all
> that is just. Perseverance is the foundation of all actions.

Because the superior man embodies humaneness, he is able to govern men. Because he brings about the harmonious working together of all that is beautiful, he is able to unite them through the mores. Because he furthers all beings, he is able to bring them into harmony through justice. Because he is persevering and firm, he is able to carry out all actions.

and further:

The Creative, by positing the beginning, is able to further the world with beauty. Its true greatness lies in the fact that nothing is said about the means by which it furthers.

The last sentence is especially important. The mode of creative activity is not bound to any form; it has no fixed character and no individual limitation. Heaven acts through the fact of its existence, not through its qualities.

The texts to the six lines of this hexagram are constructed according to the first, or "variations," type. The leitmotiv is the dragon, attributed to heaven and appearing again and again in many different forms.

The first line has for text: "Hidden dragon. Do not act." Here the light power is still down below, the dragon lies hidden under the water. Yang is already present, but has not yet manifested itself. This is a situation of considerable difficulty. To feel the radiant power, the dragon character, in one's heart, but nonetheless to lie low, is the task imposed here. Confucius has remarked about this line:

This means a person who has the character of a dragon but remains concealed. He does not change to suit the outside world; he makes no name for himself. He withdraws from the world, yet is not sad about it. He receives no recognition, yet is not sad about it. If lucky, he carries out his principles; if unlucky, he withdraws with them. Verily, he cannot be uprooted; he is a hidden dragon. [II, 12]

Confucius himself in his later years had to live out the maxims of this situation under the most distressing circumstances. He knew that he had in him the qualities for action, but influence on the outside world was denied him. We know that his adherence to the precept "do not act" finally led to success, for it prevented a premature emergence into public life that would only have made the seeds of his influence fall victim to the destructive forces of the time. His success was posthumous, and the fruits of it did not fall to him personally, but to his teaching. But it did not sadden him. This holding to seclusion in the world of darkness when no man can work effectively has always characterized the great personalities of China in situations of political decay. In this way they have been able to protect the cultural substratum of their tradition from harmful waste, so that when the day of creative activity dawned again, they could place themselves unweakened in the service of the renewal.

The situation becomes even clearer if we carry out the possibility of change inherent in the nine at the beginning and substitute a six for it. Then we obtain the hexagram Kou, Coming to Meet, a thoroughly humiliating image, that is, the image of a girl who offers herself to men. The Judgment says: "One should not marry such a maiden." That makes it clear how important it is in this situation to hold back completely and to avoid offering oneself in a characterless way merely for the sake of influence.

But the situation changes with the second line. The text to this says: "Dragon appearing in the field. It furthers one to see the great man." Here the dragon is already rising; but he is still on the level field; the possibility of influence begins, but only among his peers. It means that he has no superior position yet. The creative personality is not yet related to the time, but does have the opportunity to exert influence at a distance. He still has to go to the audience with the great man, the master and ruler, but he is no longer hindered in making his environment awaken to beauty and lucidity. Confucius has said about this line:

> This means a man who has the character of a dragon and is moderate and correct. Even in ordinary speech he is reliable. Even in ordinary actions he is careful. He does away with what is false and preserves his integrity. He improves his era and does not boast about it. His character is influential and transforms men. [II, 21]

Thus in this sphere effective action is altogether possible and suitable. Again, the picture becomes clearer if we change this line into a six. Then we obtain hexagram 13, T'ung Jên, Fellowship With Men, clinging flame under heaven. The Judgment in this hexagram promises success and says: "The perseverance of the superior man furthers." This hexagram likewise is not without difficulties; it can bring humiliation, too, if we do not know how to keep within certain limits, or if, on the other hand, we stay only in the bosom of the family. But, as a whole, it is a fine and strong image, a picture of comradeship and fellowship in action, about which Confucius says:

> Life leads the thoughtful man on a path of many windings.
> Now the course is checked, now it runs straight again.
> Here winged thoughts may pour freely forth in words,
> There the heavy burden of knowledge must be shut away in silence.
> But when two people are at one in their inmost hearts,
> They shatter even the strength of iron or of bronze.
> And when two people understand each other in their inmost hearts,
> Their words are sweet and strong, like the fragrance of orchids.
> [I, 329]

The nine in the third place shows the beginning of influence on the outside also. The creative personality begins to find an echo. Success sets in. This is a situation pregnant with certain dangers, the danger of being betrayed by success and of being pushed by mass followers into courses that are easy but disastrous. For we are not yet in the upper regions, nor are we down in the field any more, in the fellowship of like-minded people. And so the text reads:

> All day long the superior man is creatively active.
> At nightfall his mind is still beset with cares.
> Danger. No blame. [I, 7]

This is to say, only through unremitting activity can we avoid drifting off our course. At the beginning of success the greatest care is necessary. Confucius' comment on this line is:

The superior man improves his character and labors at his task. It is through loyalty and faith that he fosters his character. By working on his words, so that they rest firmly on truth, he makes his work enduring. He knows how this is to be achieved and achieves it; in this way he is able to plant the right seed. He knows how it is to be brought to completion and so completes it; thereby he is able to make it truly enduring. For this reason he is not proud in his superior position nor disappointed in an inferior one. [II, 13]

Regarding the composition of this hexagram, it is interesting to note that the leitmotiv of the dragon is missing in this line and the next.

When the third line undergoes change we have hexagram 10, Lü, Treading, the lake under heaven, a dangerous situation but one that includes the possibility of sublime progress. Courage and foresight, determined behavior, and perseverance together with awareness of danger are necessary. Therefore the Judgment says:

. . . Treading upon the tail of the tiger.
It does not bite the man. [I, 46]

But occasionally a sacrifice has to be made and the tiger's bite suffered. So it is said of the six in the third place in this hexagram, Treading:

He treads on the tail of the tiger.
The tiger bites the man.
Misfortune.
Thus does a warrior act on behalf of his great prince. [I, 48]

The nine in the fourth place of the hexagram Ch'ien shows the gateway to the upper regions. Here a decision must be taken. The creative force is about to establish itself and to take form. There are two possible ways of making the force effective: the way of the sage, who influences through the example set by the wholeness of his personality, and the way of the hero, who sets a standard in the life of men. The advance into public life, there to try out one's powers, is as possible

55

as is the further development of one's own nature. We have freedom of choice, but a decision must be made. And so the text for the line says:

Wavering flight over the depths.
No blame. [1, 7]

These first efforts that lift one above the average in human existence are necessarily wavering. Confucius says of this line:

In ascent or descent there is no fixed rule, except that one must do nothing evil. In advance or retreat no sustained perseverance avails, except that one must not depart from one's nature. The superior man fosters his character and labors at his task, in order to do everything at the right time. Therefore he makes no mistake. [II, 14]

Inasmuch as both possibilities are open, fidelity to one's own character and to one's own work, inner truth becomes the standard of decision.

It is the moment of the so-called creative pause. When this line changes we have the ninth hexagram, Hsiao Ch'u, The Taming Power of the Small. (In the oldest texts the name of this hexagram is: "The Overcoming of the Small Poison.") Here the wind blows over heaven, the image of refined cultivation of character and form. And the Judgment is:

Dense clouds, no rain from our western region. [1, 42]

The western region is the ancestral home of the Chou, the region of origin. Rain has not yet come, the decision has not yet been made. But the six in the fourth place declares:

If you are sincere, blood vanishes and fear gives way.
No blame. [1, 44]

The final break-through in Ch'ien is consummated in the nine in the fifth place. Here the dragon, absent in the last two lines, reappears and, what is more, in his full majesty. The accompanying text reads:

Flyir g dragon in the heavens.
It furthers one to see the great man. [1, 8]

Here the great character stands in the place appropriate to him, the great man is at his work. There is no more opposition. Heaven and men, gods and spirits, are in harmony. This harmonious way of acting, in accord with the time and with mankind, shows what the ruler can achieve. He flies like a dragon in the heavens. But even he is furthered by seeking advice from the great man, who in this case is of course a sage. Not until this last harmony is achieved is the whole cosmos brought into unison and each thing enabled to unfold according to its kind. Confucius says about this line:

Things that accord in tone vibrate together. Things that have affinity in their inmost natures seek one another. Water flows to what is wet, fire turns to what is dry. Clouds follow the dragon, wind follows the tiger. Thus the sage rises, and all creatures follow him with their eyes. What is born of heaven feels related to what is above. What is born of earth feels related to what is below. Each follows its kind. [II, 15]

If we change this line to a six, the success of this creative activity shows itself. We then have hexagram 14, Ta Yu, Possession in Great Measure, in which fire blazes brightly in heaven. This hexagram is one of the finest in the Book of Changes; the Judgment says simply: "Supreme success." This six in the fifth place, corresponding with our fifth line in Ch'ien, makes what is presupposed in this situation clear once again:

He whose truth is accessible, yet dignified,
Has good fortune. [1, 65]

And now the high point of the possible has been attained. The person who loses his connection with his followers and, Titan-like, keeps on striving when the maximum of influence has already been achieved, knowing only how to press forward and not how to retreat, isolates himself from the human sphere and loses his success. For what is complete cannot endure, and what is pushed to the limit ends in misfortune. Thus the text for the last line says:

Arrogant dragon will have cause to repent. [I, 8]

To which Confucius remarks:

He who is noble and has no corresponding position, he who stands high and has no following, he who has able people under him who do not have his support, that man will have cause for regret at every turn. [II, 16]

The change of this line from a nine to a six gives us hexagram 43, Kuai, Break-through (Resoluteness), that is, the catastrophe that follows a mounting of tension, a cloudburst, or break in a dam. "The lake has risen up to heaven. . . . The superior man . . . refrains from resting on his virtue." The Judgment for this hexagram expresses agitation:

One must resolutely make the matter known
At the court of the king.
It must be announced truthfully. Danger.
It is necessary to notify one's own city.
It does not further to resort to arms.
It furthers one to undertake something. [I, 250]

It is a highly dangerous situation that can scarcely be saved except through unwavering resoluteness.

And so we have completed the cycle of this hexagram. It remains to be noted that a special text is provided for the rare occasion when all six lines are transformed and the hexagram Ch'ien changes into the hexagram K'un:

There appears a flight of dragons without heads.
Good fortune. [I, 9]

For it is the way of heaven not to appear as the head or leader. The law of heaven is perceived in a complete change, and the world comes into order.

The hexagram K'un contains many of the most ancient symbols and ideas that have come down to us. In accord with its character, K'un is more Pythian and obscure than Ch'ien; its interpretation is much more difficult, one reason being that it represents the second compositional type, the mosaic. Hence in discussing it, we shall often have to content ourselves with suggestions and assertions.

K'un consists of divided lines only, and the trigrams contained in it are one and all the earth, the dark, receptive, maternal element. About this image it is said: "The earth's condition is receptive devotion." Unlike Ch'ien, there is no mention of activity here; instead, manifestation in reality, passive existence, are spoken of. The maxim derived from this reads:

Thus the superior man who has breadth of character
Carries the outer world. [I, 12]

That is to say, the accent is not on work on one's self, but on the relation to one's environment.

The Judgment belonging to this hexagram begins with the same four words as in Ch'ien. This hexagram, too, speaks of sublime success and perseverance that furthers, but with a highly significant difference; the perseverance is characterized as that of the mare, the animal form in which the earth goddess was imagined. The furthering perseverance is thus of a definite, unequivocal sort, not many-sided like the perseverance of heaven. A mare serves, is strong and swift, gentle and devoted. To quote the Judgment:

The Receptive brings about sublime success,
Furthering through the perseverance of a mare.
If the superior man undertakes something and tries to lead,
He goes astray;
But if he follows, he finds guidance.
It is favorable to find friends in the west and south,
To forego friends in the east and north.
Quiet perseverance brings good fortune. [I, 10]

Compliant subordination and calm are the qualities demanded by this hexagram. K'un takes heaven into itself and works at heaven's behest. West and south are summer and autumn, the time of ripening and harvest; they are the points of the compass to which the feminine trigrams, the mother and daughters, are assigned. East and north are the masculine regions in which one stands alone before his master, from whom one receives orders and to whom reports are delivered. K'un is assigned to the tenth month, approximately our November, the beginning of winter, when the creative energy has completely withdrawn itself.

The image accompanying the first line derives from this season:

When there is hoarfrost underfoot
Solid ice is not far off. [I, 12]

Living things are beginning to grow numb; winter's cold and death follow hard upon the frost of late autumn. This image carries a warning to heed the omens. The commentary on the line says:

A house that heaps good upon good is sure to have an abundance of blessings. A house that heaps evil upon evil is sure to have an abundance of ills. Where a servant murders his master, where a son murders his father, the causes do not lie between the morning and evening of one day. It took a long time for things to go so far. It came about because things that should have been stopped were not stopped soon enough.

In the Book of Changes it is said: "When there is hoarfrost underfoot, solid ice is not far off." This shows how far things go when they are allowed to run on. [II, 16]

Action in line with this foresight prepares for the turning point. The change of this line gives us hexagram 24, Fu, Return (The Turning Point).

The second line forms the essential nucleus of the hexagram K'un and represents its nature in the most characteristic situation. The accompanying text reads:

Straight, square, great.
Without purpose,
Yet nothing remains unfurthered. [I, 13]

Straight, rectangled, and vast are attributes of the earth, which is symbolized by the square. Earnest fulfillment of duty, never swerving from its straight course, because never in doubt about what to do, is what this line demands; and the result is inevitably a furthering of all creatures. In order to remain pure, this furtherance must never be intentional; it is the spontaneous working of nature. The change of this line into a nine gives us hexagram 7, Shih, The Army, and the image for its unswerving discipline.

The third line shows the element of devotion on the rise. The text says:

Hidden lines.
One is able to remain persevering.
If by chance you are in the service of a king,
Seek not works, but bring to completion. [I, 13]

The devoted person knows no vanity; he does not permit his light to shine forth, but conceals his "lines." The commentary on this says:

The dark force possesses beauty but veils it. So must a man be when entering the service of a king. He must avoid laying claim to the completed work. This is the way of the earth, the way of the wife, the way of one who serves. It is the way of the earth to make no display of completed work but rather to bring everything to completion vicariously. [II, 28]

When this line changes we obtain hexagram 15, Ch'ien, Modesty. The Judgment reads:

Modesty creates success.
The superior man carries things through. [I, 66]

This means to bring to completion, to serve the work.

61

The next line, a weak line in a weak place, but at the entrance to higher spheres, makes the strictest reticence and reserve necessary. The text says:

A tied-up sack. No blame, no praise. [I, 14]

One must curl up as if in a tied-up sack. Any movement forward entails the danger that a man who is intended to serve might, because of his rise, allow himself to become inflated with enthusiasm. In hexagram 16, Yü, Enthusiasm, which is what we obtain when this line changes, it is said:

Enthusiasm that expresses itself
Brings misfortune. [I, 72]

The inner beauty already intimated in six in the third place in K'un is in its perfect position at six in the fifth place. Here the weak line is in a central and strong position in the middle of the upper trigram. The accompanying text is:

A yellow lower garment brings supreme food fortune. [I, 14]

Yellow is the color symbolizing the earth and the center. Even in an exalted place, the spontaneity of inner beauty is called for, not outward adornment. The commentary says:

The superior man is yellow and moderate; thus he makes his influence felt in the outer world through reason.

He seeks the right place for himself and dwells in the essential.

His beauty is within, but it gives freedom to his limbs and expresses itself in his works. This is the perfection of beauty. [II, 28f]

The spontaneous effect of this beauty is to bring about holding together, actually the name of hexagram 8, which results when this line changes. It symbolizes the water of the earth and, applied to the state, is the symbol of the well-ordered social organization in which holding together manifests itself. The Judgment in this hexagram speaks of sublimity, constancy, and perseverance, qualities through which even those who waver are gradually drawn in.

The last line, which depicts the way the yin power comes to an end, has something sinister about it. The feminine principle comes to feel that its time is over, and instead of acquiescing in this, it gathers together the last of its power and perverts itself into a dragon. This attitude is challenged, of course, by the real dragon, and so the accompanying text reads:

Dragons fight in the meadow.
Their blood is black and yellow. [I, 14]

Black is the color of the heavenly dragon and yellow is the color of earth. Both powers suffer in this insane battle, which leads to a splitting apart. Po, Splitting Apart, hexagram 23, results when the six at the top changes into a nine. This evil situation, in which it does not further one to go anywhere, can be bettered only through generous giving.

But we must not let this last image influence us in respect to the hexagram as a whole, for it is among the most fruitful in the book. When all the lines change, that is, when K'un turns back into Ch'ien, there is added the saying:

Lasting perseverance furthers. [I, 15]

This is the everlasting steadfastness that ends in greatness.

6

The Ten Wings

We have reviewed the treasure of images in the trigrams and hexagrams of the Book of Changes, and have come to realize that these images and their designations belong to a very old stratum of culture and are in part even older than the time of the compilation of the book. Indeed, they belong to a phase of man's being when myths and symbols still gave form to his intuitions and experiences; they reveal a world in which the language of the psyche and the sense of community expressed by it had not yet been suppressed by a logical individuation. The vitality of the myths and symbols is still pristine: they still are the primary and direct expression of religious intuition and contemplation, not the secondary upsurge of too long backed-up waters that often overtakes peoples after an exhausting period of logical and analytical thought and then washes up turbid elements from the individual psyche in addition to the deep collective lore. Such secondary mythological periods have also occurred in China repeatedly. The centuries immediately preceding our Christian era, when the logical, philosophical thinking of the Chou period had exhausted itself, represent such a period of slackening intellectual vigor, in which social existence sinks back from the lucid heights of intellectuality into the depths of the psychic womb. Mythological memories came to life again, and China owes to this period poems and images which once more draw inspiration from the region of The Mothers, and an approach to political events, which, despite its forbidding aspects, was uninhibited and dynamic.

The mythological period from which the images of the *I Ching* stem is of a different sort, however. It is primary and immediate, not yet muddied by the sediment which periods of great intellectuality usually leave behind in the individual psyche. This is why the images coined are so illuminating and so generally valid. And, in order to make the Book of Changes out of those images, King Wên had only to formulate them and put them into an ordered system harmonizing with the rhythm of the cosmos. Nor had he far to go for this. The cosmos was not yet strange to him; it was not the subject of a specialized science; he lived in direct contact with its law of change, and the images were at hand, out of the store of ideas offered by the time and a living tradition.

The reaction induced by this self-contained system of images and symbols when it came in contact with the more intellectual and lucid world of Confucius speaks as much for its validity as for the breadth of vision and searching nature of this great man. Even to him, the images and names confronting him in this book were no longer all familiar. Statements coming from him and from his school show that their multiplicity and apparent irrationality caused some perplexity at his time, and that, even in that era, there were already persons to whom these images and names no longer conveyed anything. Confucius, however, was broad enough, unprejudiced enough, not to put aside with a shrug the creation of the master he so much revered; instead, he immersed himself in it until its meaning was revealed to him. Again and again he stressed the importance of studying this book, and a saying handed down to us from his school tells the way it should be approached.

First take up the words,
Ponder their meaning,
Then the fixed rules reveal themselves.
But if you are not the right man,
The meaning will not manifest itself to you.

Thus Confucius did not rework or edit the Book of Changes as he did the other ancient writings, but let it stand as it was and brought the light of his mind to bear on its contents only in appended comments.

The study of the Book of Changes by Confucius and his school produced the so-called Ten Wings, which represent seven texts or complexes of texts. Three of these are divided into two parts, hence the number ten. Unfortunately, these texts have come down to us only in fragmentary and corrupt condition. Important and unimportant matters are mingled indiscriminately; there are repetitions, and also many regrettable gaps; the titles often no longer fit the contents. In short, they form a conglomerate, apparently put together not very skillfully toward the end of the Chou era from remnants still extant, and then added to the *I Ching* as appendices. Therefore we must approach these texts with a certain caution, separating the important from the unimportant, and wherever this is still feasible, distinguishing between their various strata. What then remains does reward study; particularly in the passages where Confucius himself is speaking much can be gained from the clarity of his mind and the depth of his intuition.

A group of illuminating commentaries can be sorted out from what these writings contain and from fragments that must be pieced together from various sections. Several of these commentaries have come down to us. We have the so-called Commentary on the Images (*Hsiang Chuan*), a text that deduces a precept for the situation of the hexagram from the images suggested by the primary trigrams and in addition appends explanations to the individual lines. This commentary complex is without doubt composite. The so-called "small images" belonging to the individual lines show a philologically speculative character quite different from the often powerful "great images" belonging to the hexagram as a whole.

Another complex is the so-called Commentary on the Decision (*T'uan Chuan*), which uses the structure of the individual hexagrams to explain more fully the Judgments (=Decisions) belonging to them.

This commentary has been preserved in complete form. Less fortunate was the fate of the next complex, the *Wên Yen*, the so-called Commentary on the Words of the Text. This group represents a collection of several commentaries going back in part, perhaps, to Confucius himself. For the first hexagram, Ch'ien, four such commentaries on the hexagram as a whole and on each of the individual words of the text have been preserved. For the hexagram K'un, we have only one, and for the other hexagrams none is left. Then we have the book *Tsa Kua* (Miscellaneous Notes on the Hexagrams), which contains a brief definition of the names of each of the hexagrams, and the book *Hsü Kua* (Sequence of the Hexagrams), which is the basis for the present sequence of the hexagrams. These two books show some connection and often contain identical formulations. However, the *Tsa Kua* is in many instances unorthodox in its arrangement. Other commentaries, or fragments of commentaries, have found a place in the so-called Great Treatise, Ta Chuan. Actually, we have already made use of all these commentaries from different periods in discussing various hexagrams.

Second, we find in the Wings introductions to the system and content of the Book of Changes as a whole. These are to be found primarily in the Wing called *Shuo Kua*, the so-called Discussion of the Trigrams, which does not, however, contain any discussion of the individual hexagrams; it gives instead the derivation of the system of the Changes from the concept of tao and a detailed statement of what the eight trigrams symbolize. The train of thought in this section is clear and well founded. The content of the first part fits the intellectual climate of the Confucian period, and the imagery in the second part may possibly go back to traditions even older.

Further reflections on the system of the Book of Changes appear in the so-called Great Treatise, the original name of which was *H'si Tz'u Chuan*, Commentary on the Appended Judgments. As a matter of fact, with a few exceptions, we find no such commentaries in this treatise. It seems to have become the catchall for all sorts of pronouncements about the Book of Changes emanating from the Confucian School. Much of this material is certainly from the mouth of Confucius, and in the formulation much of it is strongly reminiscent of the *Lun Yü*, the Conversations or Analects of Confucius; one cannot escape the impression that the parts of the *Lun Yü* referring to the *I Ching* have been taken out of it and incorporated with this commentary. Other parts of the Great Treatise are clearly the work of disciples.

In addition to commentaries and passages of an introductory character, this treatise contains other important material. It offers some fundamental ideas on the value of the book and the use that can be made of it; it enters into discussions, evoked by the images, about the development of civilization; and lastly, it gives us maxims of behavior and character formation derived from the book. We must go into these three things more closely, for it is here that the fertile interaction between the rich symbolism of the *I Ching* and the lucid thought of Confucius and his school is best seen.

> Therefore it is the order of the Changes that the superior man devotes himself to and that he attains tranquillity by. It is the judgments on the individual lines that the superior man takes pleasure in and that he ponders on.

> Therefore the superior man contemplates these images in times of rest and meditates on the judgments. When he undertakes something, he contemplates the changes and ponders on the oracles. Therefore he is blessed by heaven. "Good fortune. Nothing that does not further." [I, 311f]

Devotion to the system of the Changes imparts the repose and joyous freedom characteristic of the superior man. Meditation on its images and judgments imparts the knowledge that arms him for all situations, and the augury given him by the oracle imparts the decision on his action; that is the threefold value of this book.

The first point, compliance, conformity of one's personal behavior with the laws of nature, is presented once more in a very impressive manner:

The Book of Changes contains the measure of heaven and earth; therefore it enables us to comprehend the tao of heaven and earth and its order.

Looking upward, we contemplate with its help the signs in the heavens; looking down, we examine the lines of the earth. Thus we come to know the circumstances of the dark and the light. Going back to the beginnings of things and pursuing them to the end, we come to know the lessons of birth and death. The union of seed and power produces all things; the escape of the soul brings about change. Through this we come to know the conditions of outgoing and returning spirits.

Since in this way man comes to resemble heaven and earth, he is not in conflict with them. His wisdom embraces all things, and his tao brings order into the whole world; therefore he does not err. He is active everywhere but does not let himself be carried away. He rejoices in heaven and has knowledge of fate, therefore he is free of care. He is content with his circumstances and genuine in his kindness, therefore he can practice love.

In it are included the forms and the scope of everything in the heavens and on earth, so that nothing escapes it. In it all things everywhere are completed, so that none is missing. Therefore by means of it we can penetrate the tao of day and night, and so understand it. Therefore the spirit is bound to no one place, nor the Book of Changes to any one form. [I, 315–19]

The second point, the guidance we may derive from reflection on the images and judgments, is elaborated in a series of comments on passages in the text.

The first example is from hexagram 61, Chung Fu, Inner Truth.

This hexagram pictures the wind sweeping over a lake. The ruler of the hexagram is the nine in the fifth place; he is the ruler who, by inner truth, reinforces the unity of his country as if with chains. The nine at the beginning shows the youth who is ready to accept truth with absolute commitment. The nine in the second place stands in the relationship of correspondence and of "resting upon," respectively, to these two lines. From its central position, it can contribute to its like-minded fellow below—both are nines—and above, it can proffer words of truth to the ruler to whom it is spiritually related. The text for this line says:

A crane calling in the shade.
Its young answers it.
I have a good goblet.
I will share it with you. [I, 252]

To this vivid image Confucius adds the following reflections on speech:

The superior man abides in his room. If his words are well spoken, he meets with assent at a distance of more than a thousand miles. How much more then from near by! If the superior man abides in his room and his words are not well spoken, he meets with contradiction at a distance of more than a thousand miles. How much more then from near by! Words go forth from one's own person and exert their influence on men. Deeds are born close at hand and become visible far away. Words and deeds are the hinge and bowspring of the superior man. As hinge and bowspring move, they bring honor or disgrace. Through words and deeds the superior man moves heaven and earth. Must one not, then, be cautious? [I, 253]

Another example is taken from hexagram 60, Chieh, Limitation, where living water, K'an, flows over the surface of the lake, Tui, a

situation calling for self-communion and reflection on what is going on in general below the surface. The nine at the beginning therefore demands that one have the insight not to go out of the door and the courtyard, because the seeds of a new activity have to mature further. Reserved silence is requisite to avoid disturbance of these developments. And so Confucius says:

Where disorder develops, words are the first steps. If the prince is not discreet, he loses his servant. If the servant is not discreet, he loses his life. If germinating things are not handled with discretion, the perfecting of them is impeded. Therefore the superior man is careful to maintain silence and does not go forth. [I, 248]

To remain silent willingly when the time demands it and to speak in the right way when that is required is thus an insight to be gained from reflecting on the images in the book. Words show the character of the speaker. In another passage in the Great Treatise, the following typology of speech is given:

The words of a man who plans revolt are confused. The words of a man who entertains doubt in his inmost heart are ramified. The words of men of good fortune are few. Excited men use many words. Slanderers of good men are roundabout in their words. The words of a man who has lost his standpoint are twisted. [I, 381]

As an example for the guidance of action, hexagram 28, Ta Kuo, Preponderance of the Great, is chosen. Here we have a lake that rises

up over the trees; this is an unusual situation that can bring misfortune, but unusual potentialities also. The weak six at the beginning, which rests under the burden of four strong lines, warns us to be cautious, and the text says:

To spread white rushes underneath.
No blame. [I, 120]

To this the commentary remarks:

It does well enough simply to place something on the floor. But if one puts white rushes underneath, how could that be a mistake? This is the extreme of caution. Rushes in themselves are worthless, but they can have a very important effect. If one is as cautious as this in all that one does, one remains free of mistakes. [I, 329]

The next example is from hexagram 40, Deliverance, Hsieh, which pictures thunder and rain. This is a time of liberation in which, however,

magnanimity and forbearance are indicated in order not to burden the work of deliverance with feelings of resentment arising from the past. A development of this kind can of course also place a weak person in a relatively elevated position, where he is apt to exploit for himself the advantages afforded by the time but on the other hand cannot rid himself of his petty past. And so the text for the six in the third place reads:

> If a man carries a burden on his back
> And nonetheless rides in a carriage,
> He thereby encourages robbers to draw near.
> Perseverance leads to humiliation. [I, 167]

To this Confucius remarks:

> Carrying a burden on the back is the business of a common man; a carriage is the appurtenance of a man of rank. Now, when a common man uses the appurtenance of a man of rank, robbers plot to take it away from him. If a man is insolent toward those above him and hard toward those below him, robbers plot to attack him. Carelessness in guarding things tempts thieves to steal. Sumptuous ornaments worn by a maiden are an enticement to rob her of her virtue. In the Book of Changes it is said: "If a man carries a burden on his back and nonetheless rides in a carriage, he thereby encourages robbers to draw near." For that is an invitation to robbers. [I, 167]

As the last example, hexagram 15, Ch'ien, Modesty, is cited again. This hexagram shows a mountain buried in the earth, that is, hidden wealth

which, in its modest way, brings about a reconciliation of the opposites —the youngest son in the service of the mother. The ruler of the hexa-

gram, nine in the third place, the active line that molds the whole
image, has the fine text:

> A superior man of modesty and merit
> Carries things to conclusion.
> Good fortune. [I, 68]

Confucius' word on this reads:

> When a man does not boast of his efforts and does not count his merits
> a virtue, he is a man of great parts. It means that for all his merits he
> subordinates himself to others. Noble of nature, reverent in his con-
> duct, the modest man is full of merit, and therefore he is able to
> maintain his position. [I, 330]

These are some of the guides for speech and action which Confucius
drew from meditating upon the images of the Book of Changes. Altogether, seven such examples are preserved to us. We do not know
whether or not there were more of them originally. It almost seems as
if seven were enough, because contained in them are the most important standards for speech and action: foresight, prudence, and determina-
tion. They show us the Book of Changes in its second aspect, that is, as
a book of wisdom.

Third, the book serves as an oracle. This is justified in the following
way:

> The names employed sound unimportant, but the possibilities of
> application are great. The meanings are far-reaching, the judgments
> are well ordered. The words are roundabout but they hit the mark.
> Things are openly set forth, but they contain also a deeper secret. This
> is why in doubtful cases they may serve to guide the conduct of men
> and thus to show the requital for reaching or for missing the goal.
> [I, 370]

Inasmuch as a special section will be devoted to the Book of Changes as
an oracle, we shall not pause here to discuss it.

There is, however, another section of the Great Treatise which we must not pass over, for it contains a very interesting theory of the history of civilization. It sets forth the idea that the most important cultural institutions and tools have arisen from the archetypal images of the Book of Changes. This theory, which asserts that the idea of a given tool has existed before its construction and practical use—that, in a word, our tools are nothing other than copies or, if you will, secularizations of religious archetypes and symbols—has today been brought forward again by certain ethnologists. The school of Leo Frobenius, in particular, has tried to show that the wheel, for example, is a representation of the sun. This is said to be borne out by the fact that the original wheel had thirty spokes, not because of the law of statics but because of the thirty days of a solar month. Or, to mention crasser examples of the Frobenius theory, cigars are said to have originated from incense and the umbrella from the halo.

The Great Treatise proposes derivations that are not quite so surprising. It assumes the hexagrams to be cosmic archetypes from whose structures and name images the creators of the culture of the past derived their inventions. Thus for example, nets and traps for hunting and fishing arose from hexagram 30, Li, The Clinging. The picture to be seen in

this hexagram is that of two meshes, so to speak, and its name suggests that something is to be made to cling to these meshes, to be caught in them. Then the text to the nine in the first place of the hexagram speaks of footprints running crisscross, which therefore might be entangled in the net.

The invention of the plow is traced back to hexagram 42, I, Increase.

The primitive plow, in contrast to the hoe, consisted of a digging stick that could be pushed or drawn. Hexagram I consists of wood, Sun, above, and movement, Chên, below. Earth that is to be moved is suggested by the lower nuclear trigram K'un, and the ridge of earth thrown up by the plow, by the upper nuclear trigram Kên. The hexagram as a whole brings to mind the increase of production by the plow. In a similar way, the institution of the market is explained by hexagram 21, Shih Ho, Biting Through. This hexagram presents a crowd

of people moving around in a sunny place. Its Judgment speaks of the institution of a court day, with which a market day was probably combined.

Continuing along the same lines, oars and boats, the taming of the ox and the horse, the institution of police, the use of mortar and pestle, bow and arrow, house-building, the sarcophagus and writing, are traced back to the hexagrams of the Book of Changes.

Besides the tools of our cultural activities, another section of the Great Treatise traces the structure of our character to images from the Book of Changes. Nine hexagrams showing the building of character are selected.

The first is hexagram 10, Lü, Conduct. It pictures heaven over the lake, suggesting the idea of the gradations separating high and low and,

growing out of this, social conduct. Awareness of the rules of good conduct is the sole foundation on which character can be erected in the stream of life. By correct behavior before his superiors and masters, the novice creates a sphere of harmony that can also be maintained in difficult situations—one must know how to tread on the tail of the tiger —and can enable him to reach his goal.

The second hexagram chosen is again Modesty, Ch'ien (15), under the guidance of which a man integrates with his inner nature the outer forms of the good behavior he has learned and thereby creates the "handle" of character; he brings moral law to bear upon himself and stands in reverence before him to whom honor is due.

The next step in character building is shown in hexagram 24, Fu, The Return. It is made up of one strong and five weak lines. Here we

have the first stage of individual development, the "stem" of character, still small, but the beginning of self-knowledge, of separation from the outside world. The image is thunder in the depths of the earth, symbol of the turning point.

Then follows hexagram 32, Hêng, Duration, thunder over wind. Here character gains its firmness through manifold experience. In hold-

ing firmly to his innate being, a man can develop his character until it is unified and unique.

There are still difficulties to overcome. The next hexagram is Sun, Decrease (41), the lake at the foot of the mountain. To keep one's

character from deteriorating in difficult times and to cultivate one's nature in private without striving beyond one's place, one must learn self-control—something that, once achieved, makes everything else easy.

But mere ascetic discipline is not enough for character formation. Hence there now follows I, Increase (42). This shows wind and thunder again, but in reverse order. Here character has attained fullness: it is the time of first expansion, when a man is called to perform useful labors and to do so without artifice—when there will be opportunity to learn by good example and to divest himself of his own weaknesses.

After this time of first creativeness comes the first setback, K'un, Oppression (47). The water has flowed out from the lake. This is the

time when character is tested, the time of frustration in which what one has to say is not believed. But if a man knows how to hold back his rancor, if he can keep free from all resentment, then he has withstood this test and can again find his great man, and through him, new success.

This success is shown in the hexagram Ching, The Well (48), wood over water. Nourished from below, growth sets in again. The influence

of a man's character now reaches far and wide without his having to move an inch. All the animals come to the nourishing spring, and a man gives forth without ever exhausting himself. That is the field of character. Finally it becomes clear where the right person is to be found without his ever needing to lift a finger to gain recognition.

The last hexagram in the series is Sun, the Gentle (57), the wind, appearing twice, which shows that flexibility of character should be

preserved in whatever is done and that a man should not be hardened and made rigid by external fame. Only a really mature man can weigh things on this level and, penetrating their peculiarities, preserve the unity of his character without pedantry and dogmatism. Then, through success in small things, a man can carry on his affairs, send out his decrees, and yet remain hidden and let the world go its round.

With these considerations we have touched upon some of the lines of thought which Confucius and his school contributed to the Book of Changes. Subsequent discussions of the book, it is true, have not held to these lucid heights. Nonetheless, many of the later thoughts and speculations stimulated by the Confucian commentaries are also worth the effort of following up.

7

The Later History of the Book of Changes

Our discussion of the system of the Book of Changes has brought out two aspects. We saw in it a method of divination, a way of access to the deep-lying psychic strata of the individual and of the group, the gate to the underground foundations upon which, in the East, all being and action rests. To return to this gateway has always been the prescribed way of meeting the demands of the day; these demands are not to be met with the reactions of the moment, but with a standpoint that is steadfast and timeless. We have seen the method as an early and lucid work of the human mind, consistent, logical, and cogent. The two primary numbers, one and two, and their combinations, devised according to mathematical laws, stand for an unassailable spiritual order that is completely self-contained and leaves no room for anything equivocal or halfway in character.

This clean-cut edifice of the mind is not, however, an end in itself. It only smooths the way, and the goal it leads us to is the second aspect of the Book of Changes. Here logical systematization has not raised itself before the mind like a net in whose meshes both the supra- and the subconscious are caught. It has not become a wall cutting off conscious, everyday man from his sources in his own depths and in those of the group, thereby driving him into developments that are necessarily extreme, and for that very reason lacking in duration and solid foundation. Here the spiritual system is not an independent matrix, detached and self-sufficient; it remains in its proper place in the cosmos, one link only in the chain of knowledge. In this so-to-say ancillary role, the mind leaves open what it ordinarily blocks off—indeed, it leads directly to the bedrock which supports not only it, but human existence in its entirety. The image we have of these depths, the form we give to that part which we can grasp, is not within the sphere of the intellect. Ancient memories, early crystallizations of this primordial element, help us to feel our way into its meaning.

The universality and completeness of this *I Ching* system, in which every urge born of human will and thought is assigned its place, naturally has made possible a manifold use. The clear vision which enabled Confucius and his early followers to comprehend the totality of this system has not been given to all periods. Sometimes the focus of attention was on the clear and ordered method and was linked up with all sorts of logical speculations; sometimes the depths were sounded, and then they erupted, often in disconcerting ways. The relation between the intelligible method and the unplumbed depths was sometimes fluid, sometimes rigid; each period and each personality found itself reflected in this mirror. Thus a brief survey of these later, additional interpretations not only helps us to understand the Book of Changes, but gives us an insight into the times and personalities of the interpreters.

We have seen that our book had been made the starting point of new systems: for example, of a theory of civilization and an ethic for the individual. This development continued, in line with the tendency toward systematization of phenomena characteristic of the outgoing Chou era. Especially when the *I Ching* proved to be almost the only exception to the destruction of books initiated by Ch'in Shih Huang Ti (213 B.C.), the scholars and literati seized upon it eagerly as the last tool of their profession, and so it happened that a great deal of material crystallized around this book. Contributions came from the Taoists, who thus carried forward not only the work of their great master Lao-tse, whose view of the world was very close to that of the *I Ching*, but also the work of their later philosophers. Contributions were also made by a school of natural philosophers whose symbols and systems up to that time had moved along courses diverging in part from the *I Ching*.

In this way, for instance, a different, more rigid system of the world, the system of the "five stages of change," *wu hsing*, gained entrance to the *I Ching*. This system of "five stages of change" or activating forces, that is, water, fire, wood, metal, and earth, is also very ancient, going back to the Chou era at least, and perhaps even further. The earliest combination of the two systems is to be found in the two tablets [I, 332–33], the *Ho T'u*, the Yellow River Map, and the *Lo Shu*, the Writing from the Lo River, both of which were held to have originated in mythical times and under magical circumstances, though in all probability their origin does not antedate the last part of the Chou era.

The five stages of change—with which had been co-ordinated the above-mentioned elements, and in addition the colors, tones, points of the compass, virtues, parts of the body, and everything else imaginable —were made to conform with the numerical symbols from the commentaries of the *I Ching* in these two tablets or diagrams. The heavenly one united with the earthly six and begat water, which stands in the north. The earthly two and the heavenly seven produced fire, which stands in the south. From the three of heaven and the eight of earth came wood in the east; from the four of the earth and the nine of heaven came metal in the west; while the heavenly five and the earthly ten produced the material element of earth (arable soil), which is in the center. The *Lo Shu* then takes the numbers, separates them, and, omitting the number ten, assigns one to each of the eight trigrams. In this procedure, only the central five (as the most complex of the numbers, the one that unites the two basic elements, heaven and earth: three and two) is immune from this kind of allocation by characteristics.

Originally there seem to have been texts accompanying these tablets, but except for insignificant fragments they have been lost. We have still another group of books from this period, however, reflecting a similar spirit, which were accepted as secondary commentaries on the Book of Changes. These are the so-called eight apocrypha, in Chinese *wei*, which means the woof in weaving, as against the warp, *ching*, the classic book itself. The most important of these apocrypha is the *I-wei ch'ien tso-tu*, a discourse inspired by the hexagram Ch'ien, The Creative. The following short excerpt from this apocryph will give an idea of the line of thought followed:

> The holy men of ancient times followed the yin and the yang and from them determined decay and growth; they established Ch'ien and K'un and thereby grasped heaven and earth. Thus formed things originate from the formless. But from what do Ch'ien and K'un originate? It is said (by Lieh-tsǔ): There is a primal change, a primal beginning, a primal origin, and a primal creation. The primal change is the state in which energy does not yet express itself. The primal beginning is the state in which energy originates; the primal origin is the state in which form originates; the primal creation is the state in which matter originates. When energy, form and matter are present, but not yet separate, we call this chaos. Chaos means the state in which all things still exist mixed together and have not yet separated one from another. If one looks at it there is nothing to see; if one listens to it there is nothing to hear; if one follows it, one obtains nothing. *

Change has no limiting form. Change transforms itself and becomes one; one transforms itself and becomes seven; seven transforms itself and becomes nine. Nine is the end point of this transformation. Change then transforms itself again, however, and becomes two; two transforms itself and becomes six; six transforms itself and becomes eight. One is the origin of the transforming form. What is pure and light rises up and becomes heaven; what is turbid and heavy sinks down and be-

---

*[Cf. *Tao Té Ching*, ch. 14.]

comes earth. Things have an origin, a time of completeness, and an end. Therefore three lines form the trigram Ch'ien. When Ch'ien and K'un come together all life originates, for things are composed of yin and yang. Therefore it is doubled and six lines form a hexagram. Yang in movement advances forward; yin in movement draws back. Thus yang has seven and yin eight for a symbol. A yin and a yang together make fifteen. This is called tao. Now yang transforms seven to nine and yin transforms eight to six and together they also make fifteen. Thus the sum of the symbol and that of the transformed symbol is the same. The five tones, the six sound pipes, and the seven planets are made on this pattern. The number of the great expansion is fifty. The changes take place according to it, and the spirits and genii act in accord with it. The day has ten stems, these are the five tones. There are twelve zodiacal places, there are the six tone-pipes. There are twenty-eight lunar mansions: these are the seven planets. Therefore fifty is the great gate through which things come forth. Confucius said: "Yang is three, yin is four. That is the correct place."

Fifty was the number of yarrow stalks used in consulting the oracle. In the struggle to unite the existing systems and groups at all costs, the numbers gradually degenerated from a symbol pregnant with meaning to a means for speculative, idle play. Considerable acuteness was required to formulate all these combinations and groups of combinations in a convincing way, and here and there, together with much rubbish of logical errors and banalities, we come on shining crystals whose many facets refract a ray of real meaning. Twenty-one different commentaries on the Book of Changes and a series of theoretical works, all of which are based on the apocrypha, have come down to us from the Han era [206 B.C.–A.D. 221].

Later, various schools developed. One was the so-called misfortune school. It made the complex system of relationships extremely rigid and was thus in a position to channel the relation of cause to effect along an exactly defined course. The unfortunate consequences of deviatory behavior were grouped under the five elements.

The element, wood, is correlated with the hexagram Kuan, View

(20): it is the field of behavior. Offenses against correct behavior result in the freezing of trees, or in the so-called green evil, which consists in sacrificial animals being gnawed by rats.

Fire is correlated with a passage in the *Shuo Kua* (Discussion of the Trigrams). Since fire stands in the south, it represents the ruler who sits facing south in the presence of brightness. Seeing is associated with fire. The faults that belong here are offenses against ritual, appointment of unworthy persons, dismissal of worthy ones, and listening to slander. Their consequences are fires and strokes of lightning.

Excesses and wastefulness are the faults associated with the earth; it is the field of thinking. It can bring about heart and abdominal disease and the yellow evil of dust storms and earthquakes.

Faults that go with metal are correlated with hexagram 58, Tui, The Joyous, with which speech is associated. Mouth and tongue diseases, lascivious songs for children, and all sorts of prodigious phenomena of nature, called the white evil, result from these faults.

Hearing is correlated with water. Laxness in marriage rites, the wrong relationship between emperor and people, are the associated offenses. These result in diseases of the ear and nervousness, which are called the black evil; they may cause long cold spells and dying off among animals. There is no need for us to go into all the detailed reasons given for these severe consequences. We see here the influence of schools of natural philosophy and ideas of primitive folk magic, which found cover under the broad mantle of Taoism at that time.

In contrast to these trends, another school of thought sought to perfect and sharpen the tool of entry to the *I Ching*, that is, the hexagram itself. Two methods in particular were used. The first, the *p'ang-tung* method, consisted in the co-ordination of hexagrams that are opposites in structure. Two hexagrams, the lines of which are opposites throughout, such as Ch'ien (15) and K'un (47), or Fu, Return (24), and Kou, Coming to Meet (44), were placed side by side, and from the con-

FIGURES

FIGURE 1. *Shao Yung's Sequence*

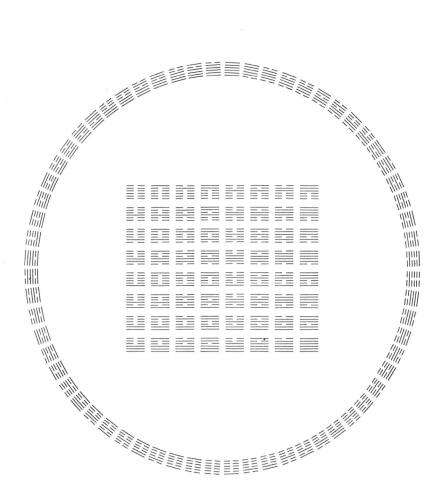

FIGURE 2. *The Circular Sequence*

trast of their total aspects conclusions were drawn for the situation as such and for the individual lines.

In the other method, called *ch'in-kua*, the hexagrams were reversed. In each hexagram its inverse was seen to be latent. The inverse of Fu would be Po, Splitting Apart (23), and the inverse of Kou would be Kuai, Breakthrough (43). Both these methods were subsequently worked

out in detail and their possible applications exactly indicated, and they certainly have some justification. The second is, indeed, often already present potentially in the sequence of the hexagrams. Both are a legitimate enlargement of the system and have continued to develop down to the present time.

In the apocrypha, we have already observed the effort to push the primal concept from which everything else was derived further back. This search for the root and cause of all things crystallized in the Han era in the word *hsüan*, the dark, the mysterious, which was established above all concepts and phenomena as the all-controlling, active essence. And from then on, all metaphysical endeavor was summed up under the word *hsüan-hsüeh*, the science of *hsüan*, or mysterious things. The idea of *hsüan* is not easily differentiated from other primal concepts, such as the concept of *I*, for instance, or of tao. Perhaps the dividing line could be drawn as follows: *I* as well as tao are the laws of becoming, under which a phenomenon organizes itself and takes its course, that is, the path of life and the law of change. *Hsüan*, on the other hand, as primal energy, is still absolutely undifferentiated; it is the primal energy monad, which is still completely neutral in respect to future developments. This *hsüan* concept led Yang Hsiung, who lived around the beginning of the Christian era, to rewrite the Book of Changes completely and give it a new form in a work called *T'ai Hsüan Ching*, the Classic of the Great Dark. It also is based on linar complexes to which situations are linked, but it contains no hexagrams; instead there are four-line complexes or tetragrams. These lines can be not only whole or divided, but also twice divided, and therefore for each place there are three possibilities giving a sum total of 81 (3^4 or 9 × 9). These four places correspond to a hierarchy of units, the first being the family, the second the district, the third the province, and on top the country. Each tetragram has nine series of texts attached to it, yielding a total of 729 texts (9^3). In many instances the store of images drawn upon is closely connected with that of the Book of Changes; in others, it seems to belong to the author's own era. We do not know whether these tetragrams and the texts associated with them are an original invention of Yang Hsiung, to whom the symbol content of the numbers three and four may have possibly been more meaningful than of two and six, or whether he drew upon another oracle book closely paralleling the *I Ching*. According to tradition, at a very early date there existed—apart from the tortoise oracle—other sources of divination along with the *I Ching*. The annals contain various oracle texts which do not appear in the *I Ching*; moreover, although hexagrams never occur in the early bronze inscriptions, occasionally one does find signs reminiscent of Yang Hsiung's tetragrams.

In all that was written and thought about the *I Ching* during the Han era one cannot fail to note a certain rigidity. Either attention was too exclusively riveted on the phenomenal world so that the priority of the images and ideas was neglected, or questions of method took precedence. It was reserved for a man of the third century to sweep aside the proliferations with a sovereign gesture and go back to the essentials. Wang Pi, born in the year 226, was only twenty-three when he died, but in the impression that he left behind he eclipsed the accumulated labors of the scholars and graybeards who had preceded him. His personal appearance alone must have been fascinating; everyone who once met him fell immediately under his spell. He is the author of the most significant commentary on Lao-tse. We also have a commentary of his on the *I Ching*, which boldly disregards philological pedantries and hairsplitting, and a series of studies of a general character putting the separate themes of the *I Ching* into the right perspective again. He too was familiar with the oracle method, but its importance did not stand in the way of the meaning; on the contrary, by means of the method he penetrated once more to the real sources of the book. His treatise on the images makes this clear. He says there:

It is the images that give the meaning, it is the words that make the images clear. To exhaust the meaning there is nothing better than the images; to exhaust the images there is nothing better than the words. The words ought to concentrate on the images, then the right words for contemplating the images are found. The images ought to concentrate on the meaning, then the right images for contemplating the meaning are found. The meaning is exhausted by means of the images. The images are exhausted by means of the words. Thus he who speaks in order to make the images clear obtains the images and becomes oblivious of the words; he who makes images that contain the meaning obtains the meaning and becomes oblivious of the images. It is like following a trail to catch a hare. Once one has the hare, one forgets the trail. Or it is like putting out wicker traps to catch fish. Once one has the fish, one forgets the traps. Now, the words are the trails of the images, and the images are the traps of the meaning. Therefore, whoever retains only the words does not grasp the images, and whoever retains only the images does not grasp the meaning. The images arise from the meaning, but if one retains only the images then what is retained are not the right images. The words arise from the images, but if one retains only the words then what is retained are not the right words. Thus only by forgetting the images can one grasp the meaning, and only by forgetting the words can one grasp the images. In fact, grasping the meaning consists in forgetting the images, and grasping the images consists in forgetting the words. Thus if images are established that exhaust the meaning completely, one may forget the images. And if the trigrams are superimposed on each other in order to exhaust the situation completely, then one may forget the exhaustion. If, then, one hits upon the types, one can make their images; if one is in harmony with the precepts, one can bear witness. If the precept is to the effect that one should act forcefully, what need of the horse? If it is to the effect that one should be obedient, what need of the cow? If the individual lines correspond to obedience, what need of saying that K'un is the cow? And if the precept demands forceful action, what need of saying that Ch'ien is the horse? If, because the horse is associated with Ch'ien, one follows only the text words in studying the hexagrams, then one has a horse, but no Ch'ien. In this way an infinity of artificial doctrines are spread abroad and it is difficult to keep them in view. Thus, if the reciprocal embodiment (of meaning and image) is inadequate to begin with, and it is then applied to the changes in the hexagrams, these become all the more inadequate. And if, in addition, one takes the five states of change into account, one immediately loses the ground from under one's feet. Even if one is clever enough to puzzle out all sorts of things by means of such subtleties, one still has not got anything from which to derive the precepts. That is the consequence of retaining the images while forgetting the meaning. Only when one forgets images and studies the meaning do the precepts emerge.*

To Wang Pi, the *I Ching* is no longer a compendium of superstition or a playground for speculation, but the book of wisdom from which precepts for action and endurance are derived. And indeed, his interpretation remained the definitive one for the next five hundred years. The better known among the T'ang commentators all followed him closely.

With the Sung period (960–1127), however, a new era of *I Ching* research begins. The exegesis of apocrypha was banned at the start of this era, because they were considered unorthodox, and Wang Pi fell into oblivion. The Sung Confucians created out of their own intellectual world new symbols and new interpretations which are not without genius and power. Nearly all of the great thinkers of the Sung period occupied themselves extensively with the *I Ching*. One of the old masters of Sung philosophy, Chou Tun-i, is the author of a treatise on the *t'ai chi t'u*, the symbol of the great pole, that primal monad in which the two forces yin and yang are shown intertwined. Out of this symbol, the imagery of the stages of change and the whole phenomenal world is derived. Another of his treatises is called the *I-t'ung shu*, the Book for the Explaining of the *I Ching*; in it he derives the principles of Sung philosophy from the *I Ching*. It begins as follows:

Chou I Lüeh-li, section 4.

Truthfulness is the root of the holy. Great is the origin of Ch'ien, from it all things take their beginning; it is the source of truthfulness. When the tao of Ch'ien alters and changes, the nature and destiny of every man takes its course accordingly. Thus is truthfulness established. The pure and the simple is the highest good. Therefore it is said: Now yin, now yang, that is tao; what makes it continue is goodness, what completes it is nature. The sublime success (the first two attributes of Ch'ien) is the penetration of truthfulness. The furthering perseverance is the return of truthfulness. The *I Ching* is great, it is the source of nature and of destiny.

Hsing and *ming*, nature and destiny or character and fate, became the two fundamental concepts of Sung philosophy. Its rational principle, or law of organization, *li*, determines the worldly course of *hsing* and *ming*, which are mutually interlocked. And the world, in turn, is an interpenetration of energy and matter. In bold phrases Chou Tun-i elaborates this idea further.

Thus it is clear that the Sung Confucians, too, had their images and their metaphysical speculation. Both, however, differ fundamentally from the creations of the Han era in the ethical note that is always sounded. Even though the Sung philosophers, like the Han, place greater emphasis on the static element, on "the unchangeableness of change," nonetheless their images are lucid and powerful; their deductions are concentrated, clean cut, and far removed from purely phenomenal analogies. These thinkers are the great idealists among Chinese philosophers, to whom transcendence is no longer something antecedent in time but an idea superordinate to phenomena.

The second of the great masters of Sung Confucianism, Shao Yung, was a speculative genius, and his philosophical deductions from the fundamental concepts of the *I Ching* are so concise and charged with meaning that it is virtually a sensuous pleasure to follow them; at the same time, they are so wide-ranging as to reach into every corner of the world. Shao Yung's mathematical exactitude led him to work out a different *I Ching* table, in which he arranges the hexagrams in a natural system.

He starts with the two primary lines, the light and the dark, then adds to each again a light and a dark line, thus obtaining four two-line complexes:

Above each of these a light line and again, alternately, a dark line is added, so that the eight trigrams stand in the following arrangement:

Continuing in the same way, he obtains first complexes of four, then of five, and finally of six lines, that is, the hexagram, as shown in Figure 1. This so-called natural order can be arranged in a sequence, one hexagram after the other, or in a square of eight times eight hexagrams, in which counting begins at the lower right-hand corner and continues through to the lower left, then starts again at the right on the second line from below and continues to the left, and so on. Finally, the arrangement can also be a circle; one half was separated and inverted in order to make it harmonize with an earlier arrangement of the eight trigrams known as the Sequence of Earlier Heaven. [1, 285] (Cf. Figure 2.) Earlier Heaven here does not signify something antecedent in time but the transcendental world of ideas—in other words, an *a priori* arrangement.

Shao Yung's schema has led to one of the most extraordinary episodes in the history of the human mind, and to this day it has never been satisfactorily cleared up. More than six hundred years after its origin, Shao's diagram fell into the hands of Leibniz through the agency of Jesuit missionaries, and he recognized in it a system that had previously sprung from his own mathematical genius. To facilitate the solution of certain mathematical problems, Leibniz had thought out the so-called binary, or dyadic, numeral system, which makes use of two numbers only, instead of ten, but otherwise follows the same principle as the decimal system. The two figures are 0 and 1. The numerical sequence of the binary system would look as follows:

1, 10, 11, 100, 101, 110, 111, 1000, etc.

In the Sequence of Earlier Heaven Leibniz now rediscovered his own dyadic system, though he had to begin with zero for the correspondence to emerge. He took the broken line for a zero, and the unbroken for a 1. Thus the hexagram Po was 1, if zeros preceding 1 are disregarded, and stood in the first place in his system; the next, Pi, was 10, that is, our 2; and so on. Leibniz placed the zero (=K'un) at the beginning of the sequence, and so Shao Yung's system corresponded point for point with the binary system, right up to the last hexagram, Ch'ien, which for Leibniz was 111111, or 63. The only difference is that this correspondence is not a direct but an inverted one, that is, in order to obtain it, one must begin at the end of the series, which serves to emphasize once more the fact that parallel cultural phenomena in East and West are as mirror images to each other! Nonetheless, the correspondence arrived at by these two great minds independently, each having started from a completely different basis, is truly an astonishing phenomenon. To Leibniz, the key to the problems before him was number; to Shao Yung, it was the hexagram. And the intellectual means by which these two kindred spirits tackled their problems took on the same form in both. For a long time Leibniz had been trying to validate spiritual truths in mathematical terms, thus making them, as he thought, irrefutable. It is easy to imagine the enthusiasm aroused in him by the discovery of this correspondence. *

With this digression we shall close our reflections on the philosophy of the *I Ching*. It should be noted, though, that Chinese thinkers did not rest content with the static images and deductions of the Sung Confucians. In the early Ch'ing era (Manchu, 1644–1911) when Confucianism celebrated its renaissance, Wang Fu-chih (1691–92) again called attention to the dynamism inherent in the hexagrams. And as late as the eighteenth and nineteenth centuries, valuable and original studies of the *I Ching* were still being written.

---

*[For a more detailed treatment, see Hellmut Wilhelm, "The Concept of Time in the Book of Changes," *Man and Time* (Papers from the Eranos Yearbooks, 3; New York and London, 1957), 215ff.]

8

The Oracle Book

We have often had occasion to remark that the Book of Changes is originally an oracle book, that is, a system of ideas and precepts from which a person needing information could, upon putting a precisely worded question, obtain the desired answer and guidance. I have endeavored to explain how this system was constituted, in what times and ideas it had its roots, and from what reservoir the answers were taken. I hope I have succeeded in showing not only that this system is so comprehensive that not only is nothing human alien to it, but also that it embraces both the patterns on earth and the images in the heavens. Thus its scope extends in two directions beyond the situations of the controllable world of phenomena. First: not only is human action guided in those surface realms in which cause and effect can be surveyed with relative accuracy, but in addition this action is based on psychic strata not immediately accessible to consciousness but nonetheless, as individual and social agents, at least equally as significant as purely external influences—if indeed, they do not surpass them. Second: the scope of personal individuation is brought back to a natural norm. The individual must adjust to the fated order of heaven and earth, and only then does the framework of reference emerge within which action is possible and is demanded. To be guided by the contents of such a system did not appear to the Chinese as a loss of freedom; they never felt it was incompatible with their self-respect to seek an example and a standard outside the limits of the ego.

The fact that this striving for guidance outside oneself was not confined to adolescence, when we, too, entrust ourselves more or less willingly to the personality of a teacher or master, but that fully developed individuals still sought precepts from a suprapersonal source and that these precepts were received through an oracle: this fact shows an awareness of personal limitations—indeed, of the limitations of human understanding in general—that may at first seem strange to us. A glance at the periods and personalities most given to the use of the oracle reveals the remarkable fact that it was most sought out in Confucian periods rather than in Taoist—ordinarily regarded as "superstitious"— that is, it was sought out in times when conscious responsible action was the watchword, not speculative contemplation or mysticism. A man who regarded development of the personality as the most important of all tasks did not need the oracle in the Book of Changes; to him it was a book whose wisdom he absorbed in quiet reflection. But when the mature individual was confronted with far-reaching decisions affecting more than his own person, he had recourse to the yarrow stalks for guidance.

Thus it is not surprising that the oracle increased again in importance during the transition from the Ming to the Ch'ing period, when Confucianism underwent a renaissance. Those schools of thought that had used the Book of Changes primarily as a point of departure for flights of speculation were severely criticized; indeed, the significance even of Wang Pi was held to be limited. The lucid perceptions of this youth continued to be held in esteem, in contrast to those of other interpreters of the *I Ching*, but it was emphasized that he had grasped but one aspect of the Changes and that he had heeded only partially the admonition of the Wings not to stray from the Book. It was deemed somewhat arrogant that he thought he could dispense with the oracle's precepts for action and somewhat slack that, although profiting in the matter of character building from his meditation on the book's meaning, when

93

it came to action (the function for which character is formed) he neglected to draw on its precepts.

In contrast to the Ch'ing Confucians, who took up the yarrow stalks with a certain reserve and awe and whose feelings of piety led them to approach the oracle only on serious and very important occasions, the people of early times consulted the oracle with complete naïveté. The oracle pronouncements handed down to us from pre-Confucian times in particular show an unfailing disposition to receive the messages emanating from this dark gateway to which people came with questions whenever the occasion arose. The auguries obtained were regarded more as an anticipation of fate and less as directives of behavior; the terms good fortune and misfortune were given the most emphasis. The oracle was consulted not only on private matters, such as a marriage contract, but also before great undertakings of the state. There is an interesting tradition according to which King Wu, founder of the Chou dynasty, consulted both the tortoise and the yarrow stalks before striking his final blow against the Shang. The tortoise prophecy was unfavorable, while that of the yarrow stalks was favorable. He is said to have obeyed the yarrow stalks, with the result that we know. This tradition mirrors the change from one era to another: the tortoise oracle was still supporting the Shang world to which it owed its great spread, while the yarrow stalks were already open to the new era, for which the other oracle had shown itself inadequate. Nevertheless, for a long time in the early Chou period yarrow stalks and tortoise were both consulted equally, and the tortoise oracle did not begin to disappear until later. The reason for this is not hard to see: the soothsayers, as a class recruited from the descendants of the Shang, assured a further period of slowly fading life to the outlived practices of their forebears.

Important oracle pronouncements of pre-Confucian times are frequently cited in historical works. Since these are primarily state records, consultations about matters of state primarily were handed down, and scarcely any private questions (such as those preserved to us on the bones of the Shang era) are known from the early Chou period. The outcome of a battle, the advisability of an alliance or of a marriage tie between two princely houses—such matters as these were in question. Frequently the answers are recorded with the hexagram and the text. Even the texts handed down from pre-Confucian times conform, as a rule, to the text of the *I Ching* as it has been preserved to us. Sometimes there are slight deviations in the choice of words or instances of recorded texts which do not appear in the present *I Ching*. Let us examine more closely one of these early oracle pronouncements in which, in addition to the positive or negative augury, a certain feeling for the course of change is already present. It concerns an event in the early part of the seventh century B.C. At that time, Li, a ruler of the small state of Ch'en, who had gained power illegitimately, consulted the *I Ching* about the fate of his young son, Ching-Chung, in order to assure himself of the permanence of his dynasty. The hexagram indicated by the oracle was Kuan, Contemplation (View) (20), and the Judgment reads:

The ablution has been made,
But not yet the offering.
Full of trust they look up to him. [I, 87]

It is a situation where the preparations for the great sacrifice have all been carried out and every one awaits the sacred ritual full of trust and faith. The Image shows wind blowing over the earth. The six in the fourth place was the changing line, and the accompanying text says:

Contemplation of the light of the kingdom.
It furthers one to exert influence as the guest of a king. [I, 90]

The change in this line resulted in the hexagram P'i, Standstill (12). Here the Judgment reads:

Evil people do not further
The perseverance of the superior man.
The great departs; the small approaches. [I, 54]

The Image shows heaven (or the princes) striving to get away from the earth.

As we see, the oracle's message was not a simple answer in a positive or negative sense; favorable and adverse influences were intermingled. The interpretation by the priest in charge has come down as follows:

When it is said, "Contemplation of the light of the kingdom. It furthers one to exert influence as the guest of a king," does this mean that he will own the kingdom (the country) for Ch'ien? In any case, it will not be here, but in another state. And it will not be he himself, but his sons and grandchildren. The light is far away and he will receive its brightness from others. K'un means the earth, Sun is wind, and Ch'ien heaven. If wind changes into heaven standing over the earth, then it is as if a mountain were there. If he has the qualities of a mountain and is illuminated by the light of heaven (or the ruler), then he will tarry on earth. This is why it is said: "One contemplates the light of the kingdom. It furthers one to exert influence as the guest of a king." The king's court is full and many guests are there. Let jade and silk be brought to him—all that is of beauty between heaven and earth. Then it will further one to tarry as the guest of a king. (The position of the weak line at the top of the lower nuclear trigram, and its relationship of holding together with the strong line over it in the middle of the upper primary trigram, suggests the idea of mutual giving and taking, which is also expressed in the Commentary *Tsa Kua* [Tenth Wing I, 387ff].) However, now we have the hexagram Kuan, View, therefore I say that it will be only his descendants that will benefit by it. The wind wanders and is everywhere on earth. Therefore I say it will be in another state. If it is in another state, it will certainly be in one whose rulers bear the family name of Chiang. The Chiang are the descendants of the officials in charge of the sacrifices to the holy mountains. The holy mountains are next to heaven. There is nothing equal to them in greatness. If Ch'ien collapses, will he then flourish in that other state (i.e., in Ch'i)?*

---

* *Tso Chuan*, Chuang 22.

The annals state that thereafter Ch'en was conquered by his mighty neighbor Ch'u, and so heaven (the prince) had to part with his country, but that the descendants of Ching-Chung gradually won recognition in Ch'i and finally mounted the throne.

Such accounts, and the circumstance that Confucius himself frequently consulted the oracle—on one occasion he was advised, to his no small annoyance, to take care of his beard—may encourage us to learn from the wisdom of the Book of Changes, but they do not help us over the difficulty of the idea that access to this wisdom is to be obtained through the manipulation of yarrow stalks. The connection between the two is difficult for us to understand. That a number or group of numbers arrived at by counting off stalks should form the gateway to such insights is something we do not readily accept. Wang Fu-chih, the greatest *I Ching* scholar of the Ch'ing era, tried to explain it as follows:

> Between heaven and earth there exists nothing but law and energy. The energy carries the law and the law regulates the energy. Law does not manifest itself (has no form); it is only through energy that the image is formed, and the image yields the number. (Image here equals idea, number is the intelligible aspect of law as embodied in the idea.) If this law becomes blurred the image is not right and the number is not clear. This reveals itself in great things and expresses itself in small things. Thus only a man of the highest integrity can understand this law; basing himself on its revelation he can grasp the symbols, and observing its small expressions, he can understand the auguries. In this way the art of the image and number (that is, consulting the oracle) comes about by itself. *

To Wang Fu-chih, therefore, number is the phenomenal form of the law, that one of its expressions in which it is intelligible. Indeed, to seek the law through numbers and to base oneself on it is a principle by no means alien to us either, although in our case it is a different kind of law we are intent on understanding and mastering. From here it is no

---

Chou I Hei-chuan.

great step to the idea that even spheres of life to which Western science has not yet applied such methods are governed by laws, indeed that the totality of life is based on law. This step was never taken in the West, though many men have intuitively striven in that direction. Leibniz is a case in point. Thus a theoretical difficulty in purely intellectual terms regarding the oracle method would not seem to exist, and we may well permit ourselves to try to understand the experiment of the Chinese as a consummation to which we in the West have not been able to bring ourselves. This much is certain, only an unprejudiced acceptance of such a possibility as a working hypothesis will yield us a clue as to whether the Chinese experiment is to be considered successful or not.

Obviously this is not a matter open to everyone. Neither can everyone follow our scientifically ascertained mathematical laws and methods; to do so one must have a gift for mathematics, that is, a special aptitude for seeing and calculating these things. The others, meanwhile, able at best only to follow these investigators in their initial findings, have grown accustomed to accepting the final results on faith, that is, untested. If we now turn to describe the initial findings of the Chinese point of departure, it is clear that to anyone coming from the outside there will be a long stretch that can no longer be easily surveyed and which everyone is free to accept untested or to reject. Only the external method can be described; the attitude of mind which achieves the results by virtue of this method cannot be taught or described.

The method, then, consists in a manipulation of yarrow stalks which yields certain numbers and groups of numbers. These numbers and groups of numbers are held to be the phenomenal form of the law governing the situation, with the help of which the situation can be understood and mastered. It was natural that yarrow stalks in particular were chosen, because they grew wild in the common which in ancient times was set apart for sacred rituals. The plant was ready to hand, it grew in a hallowed spot and no other justification was required. Since the common has ceased to play this role, it has been customary to gather the yarrow stalks from some other hallowed place, for instance, from the grave of Confucius or of Mencius.

Fifty yarrow stalks make up the set used for consulting the oracle. However, of these fifty only forty-nine are used, one is set aside right at the beginning and plays no further part. I shall not go into the speculations on number symbolism that were attached to this and to the remaining procedures; they can perfectly well be omitted from a description of the method as such. The forty-nine stalks are now divided at random into two heaps, and a stalk is taken up from the right-hand heap and set apart; usually it is placed between the little finger and the third finger of the left hand. Then the heap on the left is taken up and counted off by fours until four stalks or less remain. These are again put aside; usually they are placed between the third finger and the middle finger of the left hand. Then one proceeds in the same way with the heap on the right (counting off by fours), until again four stalks or less remain which are placed between middle and forefinger. The sum of the stalks remaining in the hand, inclusive of the first, forms the result of the first manipulation. This sum can be either five or nine, for the sum total of the manipulated stalks consists of a number divisible by four (48), plus one. Each counting off by fours must therefore yield a number of stalks divisible by four (four or eight) plus one. At the first counting off the possible result is four, three, two, or one, since the division into the two heaps was at random. If a four was obtained at the counting through of the first heap, then the counting through of the second heap, in which the number of stalks must then also be divisible by four, will also yield a four. With the addition of the first stalk the sum total is then nine. If a three, two, or one is obtained on the first counting through, the result of the counting through of the second heap brings this number up to four. In these three cases the sum total (four plus one) is five. The five obtained in this first manipulation is assigned the number value 3 and the nine the number value 2.

Before one begins the second manipulation, the stalks that formed the remainder in the first are put aside and then one proceeds with the rest as in the first manipulation. Since nine or five stalks have been put to one side, the sum of the remaining stalks is necessarily a number divisible by four. The result of counting off these remaining stalks, which again have been divided (at random) into two piles, must be either an eight or a four; the chances of obtaining either are equal. In this second manipulation, four is reckoned as 3 and eight as 2. These stalks are also laid aside and the remainder divided and counted off, when again the result must be a four or an eight, which are evaluated as above. This triple counting off yields the first line of the hexagram one is seeking, and there are four possibilities as to the character of the line. That is to say, the sum total of the number values of the three manipulations can be six, seven, eight, or nine; there is a greater possibility of obtaining seven or eight than of obtaining six or nine. Six stands for a yin line that changes, nine for a yang line that changes, while seven and eight stand for resting yang and yin lines respectively.

When the first line of the hexagram has been obtained in this way, all the forty-nine stalks are gathered together again and the same procedure is followed to determine the second line and all the others until the hexagram has been built up. In all, eighteen countings are necessary, three for each line. In interpreting the hexagrams obtained, the texts of the Judgment and of the Image and the commentaries accompanying them are taken into account, as well as the texts of the changing lines, but not the other line texts. Then all the changing lines are changed into their opposites, that is to say, the hexagram is transformed. In this way a second hexagram is obtained. The Judgment and the Image of the first hexagram define the situation in which one finds oneself; the line texts contain the specific advice it calls for, and the Judgment and Image of the second hexagram show the result that can be attained if this counsel is followed. Line texts in the second hexagram are ignored.

Beside this yarrow-stalk procedure, there is a simplified method consisting of the tossing of coins. Usually, three of the old type of Chinese coins, with holes through the middle, inscribed on one side and blank on the other, are used for this purpose. The inscription side has the number value 2 and the other side 3. One toss of the three coins yields a line. Thus the make-up of the individual line proceeds in the same way (for example, 2 +2 +3) as when the yarrow stalks are used.

As an additional clarification, the yarrow stalks for the oracle were actually counted off at the close of the lecture and the following situation was indicated:

The line —×— means a yin line that changes, and the line —ө— 'means a yang line that changes.

Thus the starting situation is the hexagram Hsieh, Deliverance (40). A singular fact is that almost all of the lines in this situation are changing

lines, although a moving line is much less likely to turn up than a resting line. Apparently a condition is indicated in which deliverance from many kinds of things is necessary.

The hexagram Hsieh does not in itself mean freedom, it means rather that the time of inhibition   the preceding hexagram is Chien, Obstruction—is disappearing and that the resolution of the difficulties has set in. "Deliverance means release from tension," say the Wings. [II, 231] The Judgment on this hexagram reads:

> The southwest furthers.
> If there is no longer anything where one has to go,
> Return brings good fortune.
> If there is still something where one has to go,
> Hastening brings good fortune. [I, 165]

In the symbolic sequence of Later Heaven [I, 288], which apparently is earlier than the sequence of Earlier Heaven, the trigram

K'un, the earth, stands in the southwest. Thus it is furthering, in these times of deliverance, to begin again from the very beginning, to return to the soil of the beginning, and not to attempt to link up with any kind of intermediate situations. The past should be cleared away, and if there is still something to be done, let it be finished quickly so that we may be ready to keep step without reservation or delay with the advancing deliverance. The Commentary on the Decision says about this:

> When heaven and earth deliver themselves, thunder and rain set in. When thunder and rain set in, the seed pods of all fruits, plants, and trees break open. The time of Deliverance is great indeed. [II, 232]

The Image for this hexagram says:

> Thunder and rain set in:
> The image of Deliverance.
> Thus the superior man pardons mistakes
> and forgives misdeeds. [I, 166]

The image of the thunderstorm derives from the two primary trigrams. After a purifying breakthrough of this kind, there is no need anymore for a self-righteous resentment that registers and passes judgment on the mistakes of the past in a small-minded way.

This is the situation delineated by the hexagram. The separate stages by which this deliverance is consummated are represented by the changing lines. The first of these is the six at the beginning, where the text says simply, "Without blame." Liberation is beginning, we are still on the border between firm and yielding. At this point nothing more can be said.

The next changing line is the nine in the second place. Here the text says:

> One kills three foxes in the field
> And receives a yellow arrow.
> Perseverance brings good fortune. [I, 166]

Here are the first obstructions, sly foxes, who, full of cunning, guard the power from which liberation must take place. They are hunted out and killed. The reward is a yellow arrow, that is, a weapon with which further deeds of deliverance can be performed. The yellow color, signifying the center and the right mean, is a warning against all excesses of passion.

The nine in the fourth place then brings us to the duties laid upon the individual by such a time. It is said there:

Deliver yourself from your great toe.
Then the companion comes,
And him you can trust. [1, 167]

The work of deliverance must also be carried through on oneself; one must free oneself from the ties dictated by custom, even if it means a radical severing, for otherwise one will not find the companions whose trust is needed in these times.

The importance of this point is shown by the fact that the next line, the six in the fifth place, the ruler of the hexagram, elucidates it further:

If only the superior man can deliver himself,
It brings good fortune.
Thus he proves to inferior men that he is in earnest. [1, 168]

This, then, is the problem of the hexagram: the deliverance of our own selves from all the shadows of the past, from all ambiguous ties and outlived habits. The challenge is not merely directed outward to the dissolution of the obstructing power, it is also inward: only if we are really in earnest ourselves can this liberation succeed.

But if we attain this attitude the last step also will be accomplished. A six at the top means:

The prince shoots at a hawk on a high wall.
He kills it. Everything serves to further. [1, 168]

In China the hawk is not considered a noble bird. It is an inferior creature, which draws its strength from the flesh and blood of other birds. Here an inferior person, having reached a high position, is the real obstacle, and his removal by the hand of one who is dedicated leads the deliverance to the goal.

When the moving lines have changed, the resulting hexagram is I, Increase (42). This hexagram, for which the way has been cleared by

deliverance, is one of the finest and most promising in the whole Book of Changes. It is understood as the sacrifice of the higher element in honor of the lower: the lowest line of the upper trigram has placed itself under the lower trigram in the spirit of service. Thus a situation develops that is full of the finest possibilities, and about which the Judgment says:

It furthers one
To undertake something.
It furthers one to cross the great water. [I, 173]

Action is again possible and promises success; even dangerous undertakings may be risked without hesitation. The image of productive activity is intensified by the fact that this hexagram was taken to be the primordial image of plowing, the simplest, most elementary form of production, which makes the bounty of heaven and the fertility of the earth useful to man.

And so the text for the Image gives the simple admonition:

Wind and thunder: the image of Increase.
Thus the superior man:
If he sees good, he imitates it;
If he has faults, he rids himself of them. [I, 174]

INDEX

Index